COMPACT
CYMRU

Wales Before 1536

Medieval Wales facing the Normans

Donald Gregory

Carreg Gwalch

ISBN: 978-1-84524-211-4
Cover design: Eleri Owen
Published by Gwasg Carreg Gwalch,
12 Iard yr Orsaf, Llanrwst, Wales LL26 0EH
tel: 01492 642031
email: llanrwst@carreg-gwalch.cymru
website: www.carreg-gwalch.cymru

Acknowledgements

The publishers are grateful to the family of the
deceased author for every co-operation in
launching this new edition.

Donald Gregory (1911 – 2006) became a
Radnor youth when his father became
postmaster at Llandrindod. He became familiar
with the remote countryside of moors and hills
and interested in its past and heritage. Later, as
a history student and teacher, his obsession
with understanding and appreciating the past
evolved to cover the whole of Wales. He and his
wife spent decades of their holidays on the
bylanes of Wales, visiting the places where
history comes alive.

*Page 1: 'The Sword of the Welsh Princes' – Gerallt
Evans' iron sculpture to Welsh resistance at Llanberis;
Below: Manorbier Castle, Pembrokeshire*

Contents

Acknowledgements   2

Foreword   4

Introduction   6

Toward Unification   10
Rhodri Mawr: Leader of Men   10
Hywel Dda: Peaceful Organiser   15
The Spread of Feudalism   20
Gruffudd ap Llywelyn, King of All
     Wales   23
Early Norman Infiltration   29

Notes and Illustrations   39

The Knitting Together of Wales   44
National awakening under Owain
     Gwynedd and Rhys ap Gruffudd   44
The Christian Church in Medieval
     Wales   50

Giraldus Cambrensis – Prelate and
     Chronicler   54
Changing fortunes under Llywelyn ap
     Iorwerth and Llywelyn ap Gruffudd   67
Owain Glyndŵr: Hero of Wales   86

Notes and Illustrations   97

Towards Union – or Annexation   114
The Tudor Triumph   114
The Act of Union 1536   121

Notes and Illustrations   125

Bibliography   128

Welsh place names   128

Foreword

Most of this book consists of a chronological outline of Welsh history from the ninth to the sixteenth centuries, from the brave attempt of Rhodri Mawr to unify his country, to the English Parliament's proffered solution to all the problems of Wales. The book is also intended to act as something of a guide to those who like to relate what they read to places they can visit; such readers will find, after the three historical parts, further sections that contain notes and illustrations, which are meant to enlighten and to entertain.

If there are readers who find it difficult to identify with events that happened long ago and to grasp imaginatively great tracts of time, they may find it helpful to try to see the past in terms of the lifetimes of people whom they may know who have had their eightieth birthdays. Try to bridge the gap between then and now, between the past and the present, by looking at the past in terms of the lives of these 80-year olds, living in succession. An 80-year-old today is separated from the time of Rhodri Mawr by only 13 such lifetimes. Once this imaginative leap has been made, it will become that much easier to grasp that Owain Glyndŵr lived about eight such lifetimes ago.

Maen Gwynedd, a boundary stone between the provinces of Gwynedd and Powys – two lands that were united under Rhodri Mawr in 855

Introduction

According to one of the many aphorisms which are credited to Confucius, the future never lies ahead of us but always comes flying over our heads from behind. Nowhere is it more necessary to remember these words of wisdom than when considering the troubled course of Welsh history in the centuries preceding the attempts of the Norman conquerors of England to extend their area of conquest further to the west. Towards the end of the fourth century AD the Romans had withdrawn their legions from Wales, where with varying degrees of success they had lorded it for nearly 400 years over Celtic tribes, who had settled in Wales 500 years before the Romans crossed the Severn and the Dee.

With no common enemy any longer in their midst, the main Celtic tribes, the Deceangli and the Ordovices in the north and north-west, and the Demetae and the Silures in the south-west and south, began to indulge themselves in the unrewarding luxury of intertribal rivalry. Each tribe sought unsuccessfully to fill the vacuum created by the departure of the Romans; there was no longer any central authority in Wales, and what local authority there was gradually became more eroded by the existing custom of inheritance, known as gavelkind, whereby a man's property at death was equally divided among all his male heirs.

Such was the situation at the beginning of the fifth century, when there was an unexpected development in Anglesey, when another Celtic tribe, the Votadini, who had come down from Strathclyde in Scotland, took possession of the island; their leader, who was believed to be a Christian, was Cunedda, who set up his headquarters in Aberffraw on the west coast of the island. At the same time, the Welsh language evolved from the Brythonic branch of the Celtic language. A few years later his grandson Cadwallon drove the Irish settlers out of Anglesey, while Cadwallon's son Maelgwn Gwynedd not only gave his name to the territory his family was to govern, but also much increased its area. Towards the end of the sixth century his efforts made it possible for his successors to extend their authority as far southwards as the mouth of the river Teifi, where modern Cardigan now stands.

Meanwhile, earlier in the sixth century, Saxon invaders from across the North Sea, who had managed to establish themselves in eastern Britain in the previous century, had tried to move further west. In these uncertain times, when fact and fiction seemed to overlap and where the one could hardly be distinguished from the other, a Welsh leader emerged, identified by some as Arthur, who succeeded at least for the time being in stopping any further incursions westwards by Saxon soldiery. The Saxon name on the inhabitants they found to the west was *Wealsch*, deriving from the Germanic for 'foreigner'; the 'Welsh' used a new name to define their land and their people: *Cymru* – people sharing the same land.

While Welsh tribes during the fifth and sixth centuries were thus struggling with their manifold problems, further east in Britain even more serious turmoil had followed in the train of the Roman abandonment of Britain. A series of invasions and large-scale migrations of Saxon peoples from north-west Europe brought Angles and Jutes and Saxons to these shores. In the course of time a number of focal points of government were developed, which stretched from Wessex in the south-west to Northumbria in the north-east. Before these quarrelling, energetic Saxons were taught by harsh experience the wisdom of joining forces to produce a unified state, which was to provide England with its first centralized government, they had been disposed to fight each other for suzerainty. The western Saxons from Wessex, along with the middle Saxons from Mercia and the northern Saxons from Northumbria, while at various times fighting each other, yet managed to find the necessary energy to drive back the Welsh, whose boundaries in former times had been much further to the east.

In the seventh century the Northumbrians for a while posed the greatest threat to the Welsh, several times between 600 and 620 mounting successful forays into the Welsh lands south of Chester. Then the pendulum swung for a while, and indeed for a short time the Welsh, who were in temporary alliance with the men of Mercia, defeated the Northumbrians in a battle deep in the heart of what is now Yorkshire. However, by 650 the Welsh were back again, defending their eastern frontier near Chester. The following century, the eighth, saw the Mercians achieving a position of military superiority over the rest of the Saxons, thereafter constituting a most serious threat to Gwynedd. It was in the last decade of this century that the Mercian king, Offa, caused his dyke to be built, which was to become the first recognisable political boundary between the Saxons and the Welsh. Offa died in 796 and Mercia soon fell into a state of confusion, of which Wessex, the kingdom of the West Saxons, soon took full advantage. The Wessex king, Egbert, who ruled from 802 to 839, defeated the Mercians in battle in 825; thereafter the men of Mercia had to do homage to Wessex. Indeed, before his death in 839, Egbert received homage from every ruler in England, thereby becoming the first king of a unified England.

To return to the eighth century, on the mainland of Europe significant developments had been taking place; the chaos and disorder, which centuries before had followed the break-up of the Roman Empire in the west, had gradually been replaced by a return to some semblance of central government in various parts of

Offa's Dyke near Presteigne, which helped to define the new land of Cymru – Wales

western Europe, which at the very end of this century culminated in the creation by Charlemagne of an Empire in the west; on Christmas Day in 800, in St Peter's in Rome, the Pope crowned Charlemagne Emperor. His power, which, as will be seen, was but briefly exercised, stretched from the Pyrenees in the south-west to the Baltic in the north-east and to Rome in the south.

Meanwhile, back in Wales, attention must now be drawn to the terrible impact made on the country by the most formidable external threat of all, that posed by the sea raids of the Vikings.

These daunting giants from the north, like the Romans before them, have had a bad press! Just as the Romans came and saw and conquered in the public mind, so did the Vikings spread terror far and wide when they crept silently up the creeks on dark nights. Admittedly the Romans were military conquerors and the Vikings were blood-thirsty sea raiders, but there was much more to the Romans than fighting and much more to the Vikings than raiding.

Who indeed were these Vikings, and where did they come from? Their far-off homes were in the northern lands, where today live the Norwegians, the Swedes and the Danes. In some parts of Europe they were known as the Northmen or the Norsemen or the Danes, and in other parts simply the Vikings, but to every one they were, one and all, raiders and destroyers, restless and ruthless seamen, who were also wonderful navigators. Their various expeditions took them to Spain, to Italy, to Iceland and to Russia, to France and to our own islands. Charlemagne, whose newly-established empire in the west had been based on Christian law and order, died in 814 and, although the central core of his possessions survived his death, the rest of his empire very quickly crumbled and disintegrated. The men from the North saw their chance and took it.

Their most spectacular conquests were in the east of Europe but they also raided and settled in the Faroes, Shetland, the Orkneys, in the Hebrides and in various parts of mainland Scotland, in Northumbria, Cumbria and in Lancashire, in the Isle of Man and in Ireland. Of many of these raids very little is known; enough of the consequences have survived, however, to realise that the very fabric of civilisation in western Europe, already greatly weakened, was very nearly ruined by the Vikings. This is particularly true of Ireland, where the impact was probably the severest of all. Ireland, which had escaped Saxon infiltration and conquest, was enjoying a secure and trouble-free existence, with a separate and exciting culture, when the Viking raids began. This golden age of Ireland came to a sudden and terrible end in 853, when the Vikings, as the result of an overwhelming military victory, became the lords of Ireland. This was the terrifying challenge with which Rhodri was to be confronted nine years after he had succeeded his father as ruler of Gwynedd in 844.

Toward Unification

Rhodri Mawr: Leader of Men

This chronicle proper begins in the year 844 with the accession to power in Gwynedd of Rhodri, later to be accorded the additional name of Mawr (*mawr* = great). With the benefit of hindsight, it can now be seen that the movement towards unification in Wales began in the middle of this ninth century, when a train of events was set in motion which was to lead, after many remarkable vicissitudes 700 years later to the passage through Parliament in Westminster in 1536 of a bill that forcibly joined Wales to England. This turn in events was the more curious – and the less probable – because the King of England who initiated this course of action, Henry VIII, was himself partly Welsh: indeed, he was the son of the Welshman, Henry Tudur, who had wrested the crown of England from Richard III at the Battle of Bosworth in 1485, before making himself King of England as Henry VII.

It would be misleading, however, to suggest that in 844 Rhodri and those who supported him ever thought of themselves as primarily Welshmen, Rhodri probably saw himself as the leader of the men of Gwynedd, who controlled the destinies of northern Wales. Although Wales in the ninth century had a linguistic and cultural unity and had been recognised as a country since Roman times, it was not politically unified – the land west of Offa's newly-dug dyke consisted of a number of more or less separate political units; all this happened at a time when Egbert, the grandfather of Alfred the Great, had already become the king of a unified country.

Rhodri took over the reins of government in Gwynedd in 844 on the death of his father, Merfyn Frych, who had ruled Gwynedd firmly for nineteen years. This Merfyn was descended on his mother's side from the great Maelgwn Gwynedd, the great grandson of Cunedda himself, who had migrated from Strathclyde to Anglesey in the early years of the fifth century. Merfyn greatly strengthened his position when he married Nest, the sister of the ruler of Powys, Cyngen. A few years previously Cyngen had caused to be erected in a field

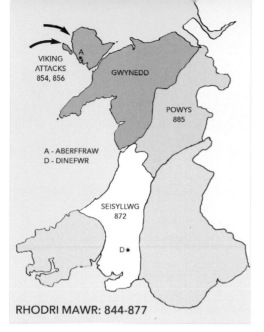

VIKING ATTACKS 854, 856

GWYNEDD

POWYS 885

A - ABERFFRAW
D - DINEFWR

SEISYLLWG 872

RHODRI MAWR: 844-877

This alliance between Gwynedd and Powys became politically of far greater significance in 855, when Rhodri's uncle, Cyngen, the Prince of Powys, who died while on a visit to Rome, bequeathed his domain to his nephew. This enabled Rhodri to become the first Welshman to rule both Gwynedd and Powys, and thus become master of most of the north, the east and the central parts of Wales. Furthermore Rhodri, like his father before him, greatly added to his dominions as a result of a prudent marriage. His wife was Angharad, the sister of Gwgon, the ruler of Ceredigion in the far south, who during his reign had managed to annex Carmarthen, creating the new kingdom of Seisyllwg. Angharad in addition bore her husband no fewer than six sons, three of whom were later to figure prominently in the future government of Wales. In 872 Gwgon died, leaving to his brother-in-law in the north Seisyllwg, thus making it possible for Rhodri to become ruler of north, central, east and of a great part of southern Wales. Gwynedd, Powys and Seisyllwg became under Rhodri's careful guidance a loose association of provinces, which provided in later years a useful pattern for those who looked ahead longingly to the time

near Llangollen a memorial cross in honour of one of his forebears, a cross known as Eliseg's Pillar, which today, even in truncated form, constitutes one of the most important historical monuments in the whole of Wales. The political consequence of this marriage between Rhodri's father and a Powys princess was very considerable, as it freed Gwynedd from the irksome responsibility of defending itself against Mercian attacks from the other side of Offa's Dyke.

when a unified Wales might become a reasonable goal.

Something has already been said about the dreaded Vikings, some of whose most successful sea raiders had in 853 set themselves up in Dublin, from where they were soon to launch ferocious attacks on Wales. A glance at the map of Wales today, looking in an anti-clockwise direction, will give the reader some idea of the extent of this Viking threat, and some understanding of the menace implicit in 150 years of unremitting fear by night. This is underlined by the Viking names, which date from these uncertain years, to which the Great Orme and the Skerries, Bardsey and Fishguard, Skomer and Skokholm, Lydstep and Tenby, Worm's Head and Swansea bear historic witness. Rhodri was the first ruler to have to bear the responsibility for warding off these murderous assaults along the long, indented coastline of Wales, the raiders almost permanently poised to swoop from their Irish bases upon unprotected settlements.

Nine times did Anglesey feel the full force of Viking invasion, the first time in 854, the last in 987, when 1,000 defenders perished and twice that number were carried off into captivity. In these years of dread Holyhead, Aberffraw (the seat of Gwynedd's government) and Penmon were all victims of this northern fury. The last of all the very many Viking raids on Wales was mounted against St David's in 999, when the bishop fell victim to a murderous attack. No proper understanding of Welsh history in that troubled century and a half is at all possible unless seen against this tumultuous background of continuous fear of a sudden Viking foray from an Irish base.

Rhodri, alarmed at the ever-increasing might of Mercia in the east, and alerted by news of the first Viking attack on the coast of Anglesey in 854, girded himself for the coming fight; it is unfortunate for posterity that no contemporary account of these raids survives, but what little is known shows that in a subsequent attack on Anglesey in 865 the Viking leader, Gorm, was killed in battle by Rhodri. News of this achievement comes from a congratulatory message handed to Rhodri at his court at Aberffraw by the diplomatic representative of the King of the Franks, expressing the gratitude of his master, King Charles the Bald, whose dominions were likewise being threatened by similar Viking violence. It is interesting to note from this and other such contemporary references that there appears to have been at this time civilised court life in Aberffraw, where emissaries from foreign governments participated in peaceful and scholarly relationships with the leading men of Gwynedd. Many other Viking raids Rhodri had to endure; sometime he drove the marauders off, sometimes he had to withdraw in the face of a ruthless and determined enemy. His great achievement was so to limit the success of Viking raids that they were never able to follow up their raids by establishing lasting settlements, as other Viking raiders succeeded in doing in other parts of Britain.

By the middle of the 870s, by which time Rhodri had shouldered the burden of government for thirty years, he had indeed achieved much, as he had succeeded in holding in check the ambitious men of Mercia and in keeping the rampaging Vikings from proceeding far inland, while at the same time managing to offer well-ordered government to his subjects in the three widely-separated provinces of Gwynedd, Powys and Seisyllwg. By this time, however, he must have begun to wonder what would happen to his dominions after his death. Reference has already been made to the contacts enjoyed by Rhodri in his court with representatives of other countries, such as the Kingdom of the Franks, whose king, Charles the Bald, was the grandson of Charlemagne. From contacts such as this Rhodri had learned of Charlemagne's worries about the future of his empire after his death. Charlemagne had in consequence called a conference in 806, at which the decision had been taken for his empire to be divided at his death between his three sons.

In 876 Rhodri called a similar meeting of his family and advisers at Dinefwr Castle in Seisyllwg, which stands on a hill to the south-west of Llandeilo, commanding the Tywi valley. The reason for the meeting was soon made clear to all; Rhodri, taking a leaf out of Charlemagne's book, wanted to arrange for the future stability of his dominions, while he was still in a position of authority to arrange it. He had six sons and he was fully aware of the weakening political effect that would follow an equal division of his property at his death, for which the application of the inheritance law of gavelkind would call. At

Dinefwr Rhodri selected the three strongest of his sons to inherit his property, along with the inseparable positions of authority that went with such bequests. The government of Gwynedd was to go to Anarawd, of Powys to Merfyn and of Seisyllwg to Cadell. (Readers of Giraldus Cambrensis are warned that the chronicler mixed up these inheritance arrangements, giving Gwynedd to Merfyn and Powys to Anarawd.) The reactions of the other three sons, who were to lose their inheritances, can but be guessed at. The validity of these arrangements was to be put to the test much sooner than could have been predicted at Dinefwr, as Rhodri was killed in battle the very next year, in 877; it is thought, though not known for certain, that the skirmish was with the Saxons.

Six years previously, in 871, Alfred had become King of Wessex; he, like Rhodri, had the Viking menace on his doorstep. After considerable successful settlement in Yorkshire and in the north-east, the Vikings, who are referred to as Danes in English history, turned their attention to Wessex, where for a long time Alfred managed to hold them off. In 878, after a fiercely-contested war, Alfred and the Viking leader, Guthrum, made an agreement whereby Alfred recognised the Danish occupation of the north of England in return for Viking recognition of Alfred's independence in Wessex. This division of the country into the Danelaw in the north and Saxon independence in the south, which lasted for 100 years, freed Saxon hands for future interference in Welsh affairs.

It is of some interest to observe that in the histories of England and Wales, only Rhodri and Alfred, apart from Llywelyn, have ever acquired the title of the Great – Alfred the Great and Rhodri Mawr. In this context there is no cause to examine the reasons for Alfred's title, though clearly his stubborn and successful resistance to Viking aggression must have played an important part. Rhodri's claim to the honour is probably due to three things: his unrelenting opposition to the Vikings, the outcome of which was that the invaders nowhere in Wales succeeded in gaining a permanent foothold; his political foresight in trying to unify his country; and his undoubted success in giving cultural leadership to Gwynedd, evidence for which was provided by the highly-civilised nature of court life at Aberffraw. Rhodri

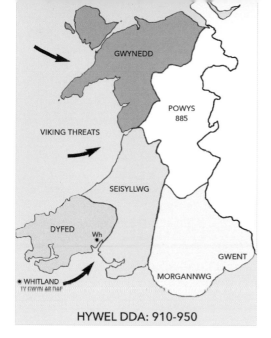

HYWEL DDA: 910-950

Gwynedd for nearly 40 years, made a ceremonial visit to Alfred's court, a controversial decision, which served to underline the strength of Alfred's position as the successful champion of the Christian cause against the Vikings; Cadell, who inherited Seisyllwg, was eventually succeeded in 910 by a famous son, Hywel Dda.

Hywel Dda: Peaceful Organiser

Rhodri's praiseworthy attempt to unify his country by making himself master of Gwynedd, Powys and Seisyllwg came to nothing in 877 when he died; though the new rulers were all brothers and the great man's sons, their three provinces were separately ruled until 904, when Merfyn, the King of Powys, died; his lands then passed to Anarawd, so that Gwynedd and Powys were once again joined together. Six years later Cadell, the King of Seisyllwg, also died, leaving instructions for his lands to be split up between Hywel (at this time known as Hywel ap Cadell) and his younger brother Clydog. Thus in 910 with Hywel and Clydog ruling a divided Seisyllwg, and their uncle Anarawd in charge of Gwynedd and Powys, with a

Mawr is regarded by some as the greatest of all Welsh kings; faced by the dual threat of Saxon might in the east and Viking terror in the west he strengthened and unified Wales. He founded a dynasty which was to become the ruling family both in northern Wales and the south.

The arrangements made in 876 at Dinefwr were duly carried out; Merfyn acquired Powys, Anarawd Gwynedd, and Cadell Seisyllwg. Anarawd, who was to rule separate king lording it over Dyfed (roughly speaking, modern Pembrokeshire) and, with other princes responsible for the separate government of Morgannwg and Gwent, Wales was once again politically fragmented, and as such a potential target for the ambitions of men east of Offa's Dyke.

At the very time when this future Hywel Dda was setting out on his momentous journey as ruler of a part of Seisyllwg, significant developments were taking place in the activities of the Vikings on the mainland of Europe. In 911 the King of France, Charles the Simple, the grandson of the King of France who had set up diplomatic relationships with Rhodri's court at Aberffraw, gave permission to a band of Northmen to settle on the north coast of France, just north of Brittany. Their leader was Rollo, who proceeded to call their settlement Normandy and began to introduce the Christian religion to his Vikings. For some years this Christian Viking kept to his Scandinavian traditions, but gradually at the same time assimilated some of the culture of France, their chief city Rouen becoming in the process one of the most enlightened places in Europe. This powerful combination of Viking virility and Latin culture was in the fullness of time to pose a considerable threat, as the Saxon leaders of England were to discover in the middle of the eleventh century and the people of Wales not very long afterwards.

Before embarking upon an account of Hywel's career, it is necessary to alert the reader to the several respects in which his actions and policies differed fundamentally from those of his illustrious grandfather. Rhodri, it must be remembered, at all times stood firm against his enemies, be they Vikings or Saxons, taking up arms against them when circumstances dictated; the consequence was that the name of Gwynedd came to be feared by its enemies and north Wales came to be associated with the leadership of Welsh affairs. Hywel, by contrast, will be seen to have been above all a very gifted organiser and with it a man of peace. In his forty years of political power he greatly increased the lands he governed, until he too, like his grandfather, ruled most of Wales, the pendulum of power in the process swinging decisively from north to south, from the suzerainty of Gwynedd to that of Deheubarth. The means by which he achieved this great position in Wales was by establishing a firm understanding with the western Saxons, whose sphere of influence at that time was widened vastly from Wessex to the greater part of England. Hywel became a strong, though junior, partner in this arrangement with the Saxons, first with Alfred's son, Edward the Elder, and then with Alfred's grandson, Athelstan. Part of the justification for this political pact was provided by the ominous increase in the ferocity of Viking raids at that time in southern and western Wales. In addition there were many Welshmen who felt very much indebted to the Saxon king for rescuing the Bishop of Llandaf, after he had been carried off by the Vikings.

At his accession, as has already been mentioned, Hywel had had to share Seisyllwg with his younger brother Clydog; he bided his time, unlike his cousin Idwal of Gwynedd, who on his father, Anarawd's death in 916, not only took over his father's kingdom but added Powys to it. Two years later, in 918, cousin Idwal accompanied Hywel and his brother Clydog across Offa's Dyke, where all three Welsh rulers paid homage to Alfred's son, Edward the Elder. Thereafter Hywel had

no occasion to worry about any threats from the Saxons. In 920 Clydog died, enabling Hywel to take over his brother's share of Seisyllwg; shortly afterwards Hywel imitated the examples set by his grandfather, Rhodri, and by his great grandfather Merfyn Frych, and made a very prudent marriage, which served greatly to strengthen his position in south Wales. His wife, Elen, who was the daughter of the last King of Dyfed, brought as her dowry Dyfed, which, when joined to Seisyllwg, became known as Deheubarth. Hywel thus became, without having to undergo the rigours of a military campaign, the ruler of all south-west Wales.

Hywel's English overlord, Edward the Elder, died in 925; in the following year his son, Athelstan, who had succeeded his father on what was virtually the throne of England, summoned Hywel and Owain, the prince of Gwent, to attend him at Hereford where, in addition to making an agreement to regard the river Wye thereabouts as the legal boundary between Welsh and Saxon lands, Hywel and Owain also paid the required homage to the new king. Thus it was that the grandson of Rhodri the Great did obeisance to the grandson of Alfred the Great. Vassal though Hywel had certainly become, it is perhaps a curiosity of history that he alone of Welsh kings issued his own coinage; silver pennies of his reign, bearing the superscription *HOWAEL REX*, were minted in Chester, specimens of which may still be seen in the British Museum.

Not long after this historic meeting at Hereford, in 928, Hywel, greatly daring, went on pilgrimage to Rome; he travelled there, secure in the belief that his frontiers would not be violated by Saxons in his absence. He probably knew that the great Wessex leader, Alfred the Great, whom he had so much admired when he was a young man, had himself twice visited Rome. Once in Rome, Hywel proclaimed himself to be the King of Wales, a claim that he could have better substantiated some years later, by which time he had managed to annex both Gwynedd and Powys. Nevertheless, even in 928 he clearly was the strongest ruler in Wales and as such best equipped to represent Welsh interests in Rome. There is, too, some reason to suppose that uppermost in his mind in deciding to go to Rome was the wish to narrow the gap that had widened in recent centuries between the Church of Rome and the Celtic Christian church in Wales. As a result of this Roman interlude Hywel's reputation back home in Wales went up by leaps and bounds.

It is an irony of Welsh history that the posthumous title Hywel Dda (*da* = good) was awarded to a Welshman whose undoubted political success must largely be attributed to close co-operation with the hated Saxons, to whom he was even prepared to render homage; however, it has to be stressed that although many of his contemporaries saw the wisdom and indeed the necessity for such a working arrangement with Wessex at that particular time, Hywel's high standing with his fellow countrymen was mostly due to a course of action which he set in motion shortly after his return from Rome, when he called an assembly at Whitland.

Hywel is still regarded above all as the great lawgiver of Wales in the Middle Ages, a reputation that stemmed from decisions taken at Whitland, probably in 930. By the tenth century Hywel found in the various parts of Wales under his jurisdiction a great many customs and practices that differed considerably from each other. Such codes of behaviour, and the attitudes of those in authority to breaches of them, varied so fundamentally that something drastic had to be done. As medieval society generally began to settle down and its institutions crystallised, this problem frequently presented itself. Hywel's solution of calling an assembly to deal with the matter was by no means an uncommon practice. Hywel's contemporary and overlord in Wessex, Athelstan, who ruled from 925 to 940, may well have influenced Hywel at this time, as he too did much to regulate and make uniform differing legal customs and practices in Wessex, and elsewhere in England where his writ ran.

To Whitland (original Welsh name *Hendy-gwyn ar Daf* – the old white house on the Taf) were summoned leading members of the clergy and also six representatives, chosen from each of the local districts throughout Hywel's extensive kingdom. This collection of leading ecclesiastics and laymen was given just 40 days in which to consider the whole conflicting body of law in their different localities and by amendment, improvements and regulations, to produce a unified and codified system of law.

There are inevitably large gaps in our knowledge of what actually happened at Whitland in 930, historians having to depend upon 35 manuscripts, which have survived from the thirteenth century. These books all deal with legal matters and they all claim to derive their authority from the conclusions reached at Whitland, but the 300-year interval between the deliberations at Whitland and their chronicling in the thirteenth century makes detailed information difficult to gather as well as introducing a certain element of doubt. It does seem, however, that all levels of law and custom were deemed to be within the delegates' terms of reference, proof of which is provided by the consideration of such trivial subjects as forms of precedence at Court, and such momentous matters as proof of guilt being thereafter required by evidence, rather than by trial by ordeal as previously.

What is very clear is that before the Whitland representatives dispersed, the accepted codification had been written down, thereafter to become the law of Wales. Something of the high regard the coded laws gradually acquired can be deduced from the fact that when in 1284 the English king Edward I wanted his Welsh adversaries to accept the provisions of the Statute of Rhuddlan, he told them that he had used Hywel's laws as the basis of all future law in Wales.

The Whitland triumph marked the highwater mark of Hywel's reign: four years later he was summoned by Athelstan to attend his court at Winchester, where he was required to countersign several charters, to which the description 'sub-king' was appended after his signature. In 942, back home in Wales, Hywel realised his political ambition, as he was able virtually to unify Wales; in that year Idwal of Gwynedd, who in 916 had annexed Powys, died in battle against the Saxon men of Mercia. Power in Gwynedd then passed not into the hands of Idwal's son, but into those of Hywel, who thus for the remaining eight years of his reign and life ruled the whole of Wales, save for the small but independent princedoms of Morgannwg and Gwent.

Of Hywel Dda as a person little is known; that he was wise and very shrewd and diplomatic, events in his reign bore out. He was, too, an exceptionally able organiser and, above all, a man of peace. His death in 950 marked the end of a period; the precarious unity of Wales, for which Rhodri and his grandson Hywel had struggled for so long in their vastly different ways, proved very short-lived, as Hywel's reign was almost immediately followed by political fragmentation, with relatives fighting tooth and nail for the succession of the constituent parts of Hywel's kingdom. Soon, alas, the Welsh world fell apart again; in the century that followed no fewer than thirty-five Welsh rulers died violent deaths at the hands of Vikings, Saxons, and also, it has to be admitted, at the hands of fellow-Welshmen. This sad decline in Welsh fortunes will have to be seen in the next section against the background of political turmoil, east of Offa's Dyke, where renewed land attacks by the Northmen for a time threatened to put the clock back there too.

The Spread of Feudalism

The fact that Welshmen from Deheubarth and indeed from other parts of Wales were having to pay homage to Wessex Saxons, a practice which may well shock many Welsh readers today, calls for explanation. In the early years of the tenth century the river Wye at Hereford and above, which was the acknowledged boundary between Wales and West Saxon lands, also marked the western frontier of feudalism. The troubled history of Welsh and Saxons in the century that lapsed between the death of Hywel Dda in 950 and the successful Norman conquest of England has to be studied against the background of this new and fast-growing form of social organisation.

The word feudal today is often used as a term of abuse; it is an adjective reserved to describe the behaviour and attitudes of those of an arrogant and authoritative disposition. Such a usage is historically inaccurate because although it is true that feudalism rather outstayed its welcome in western Europe, for a very long time it served society well, enabling it to take its first faltering steps towards recovery after the darkness descended with the fall of the western Roman Empire. Admittedly there was nothing progressive about it, but then progress is hardly to be expected when mere survival is a goal. When tumbling down a steep scree, it is enough for the climber if he can stop his fall. Feudalism enabled man to do just that.

The very foundations of European society had been rocked by the barbarian invasions. In the fifth century AD, when the long-established empire of Rome collapsed in the west, the vacuum thus created was temporarily and mercilessly filled by a succession of marauding tribes from the east; they descended into Europe, they looted and they left, leaving behind them a desert. The course of history is not by any means an upland march towards Utopia; at best it is a series of fits and starts – two steps forward and one step back, in the view of an optimist. European civilisation was certainly pushed back a very big step when Goths and Vandals and finally the terrible Huns poured in, laying waste far and wide before disappearing back into the mists of Asia.

What became known as feudalism was really the attempt made by the survivors of these misfortunes in western Europe to adjust to the ruinous situation that faced them on the morrow of European devastation. *Homo sapiens* is a resilient species. The social and political units that slowly began to appear had a rural basis, as the towns had suffered most at the hands of the invaders. Up and down the mainland of Europe similar patterns of development probably emerged quite independently, based on the ownership of land. Everywhere security was the paramount need, because no-one knew when the next threat from Asia might materialise. The legal definition of feudalism as the parcelling-out of land with authority gives a fair and reasonable description of how this regrouping of social life began. In simple terms, owners of large areas of land found it prudent to give parts of it to men whom they could trust on certain conditions. Such a piece of land was called a 'fief' and was said to be 'infeudated'. The vassals, i.e. those who received the land, in return acknowledged the authority of the overlords, pledged their homage to them, promised to attend their masters at court in peacetime and to accompany them to war, when the occasion arose. The process of subdivision of land often went much further; fiefs were subdivided and sometimes further subdivided; it was known as 'subinfeudation' and was particularly common in France. Thus the land was parcelled out and authority delegated, but if the owners of the land felt themselves insecure, so did the majority of the rest of the population who were at the bottom of the pile.

The peasants were hungry and frightened; in their search for food and security they too managed to fit into the feudal pattern of society. The peasant 'commended' himself to the nearest landowner, who may have been the overlord himself or one of his infeudated vassals, or even a subvassal. It mattered not to the peasant, who agreed to work for his lord in peacetime and to take up arms and fight for him in war, in return for which he received the priceless boon of food and protection for himself and his family. Feudalism was the product of these two complementary tendencies, infeudation and commendation. Thus it was that the social life of Europe was gradually restored on a sound and realistic basis.

By the ninth and tenth centuries the greater part of western Europe had become feudal. Although the depredations of Goths and Vandals and the like were not felt in these islands, a very considerable vacuum opened up here after the Roman writ ceased to run in the fifth century. The struggles that followed, as various tribes crossed the North Sea from Germany and Denmark, eventually gave way to a more settled order, which was partly stabilised by the acceptance of social organisation based on land tenure. The most-highly developed feudal country in Europe was France, and it is worthwhile to note that when the Vikings secured their first

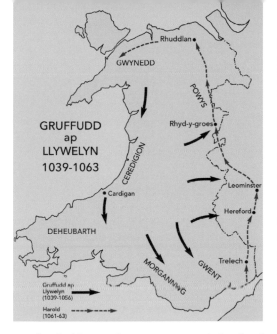

GRUFFUDD
ap
LLYWELYN
1039-1063

GWYNEDD
Rhuddlan
POWYS
Rhyd-y-groes
CEREDIGION
Cardigan
Leominster
DEHEUBARTH
Hereford
MORGANNWG
GWENT
Trelech

Gruffudd ap
Llywelyn
(1039-1056)

Harold
(1061-63)

foothold on the western mainland of Europe in 911, Rollo, their leader, technically became a vassal of a French overlord and thus was the first Viking to have been caught up in the feudal structure of society.

As a belated postscript to an account of the career of Hywel Dda it has to be stated that Wessex in the reigns of Edward the Elder and of his son, Athelstan, with both of whom Hywel had considerable contact, became increasingly more feudal in its organisation as more and more peasants, in their search for food and protection, pledged their support to their rulers.

One final point must be made: it would be an anachronism to think of Hywel and his supporters as thwarted nationalists, as full-blooded Welshmen frustrated and humiliated by the need to bend the knee to aliens. This sort of national awareness still belonged to the future. He was a son of Seisyllwg, with family roots in Gwynedd, who in his passionate search for peace for the people he ruled, expanded and strengthened his lands.

Gruffudd ap Llywelyn, King of All Wales

The years from 950 to 1040, that is to say from the death of Hywel Dda to the emergence of Gruffudd ap Llywelyn as the leader of Wales and to the death of Hardicanute, the last Danish King of England, were indeed unsettled; rulers were killed, territories changed hands and Vikings crept up Welsh creeks at night with ever-increasing ferocity and very considerable success. In 987 Anglesey again suffered Viking invasion, and between 982 and 999 St David's was four times attacked. On the last occasion the

Bishop himself was murdered: one Morganeu, who, if Giraldus Cambrensis is to be believed, was the very first Bishop of St David's ever to taste meat!

In most places in those years, confusion reigned supreme, until out of those mists there gradually took shape two larger than life figures whom destiny seems to have marked down as foemen, worthy of each other's steel: Gruffudd ap Llywelyn and Harold, the Saxon Earl of Hereford. Until the appearance of Gruffudd there was no Welshman since Hywel's death strong enough to emulate his example and that of Hywel's famous grandfather, Rhodri. Hence the north, the centre and the south of Wales remained disunited and therefore too weak to resist any pressure from outside, let alone to be able to stand up and speak with one voice for the whole of Wales.

Hope had briefly flickered into life in 986, when Hywel's grandson Maredudd ap Owain was ruler of Gwynedd and Deheubarth, but as he failed to conquer Powys, that hope soon faded away, his own nephew in Powys summoning the readily available assistance offered by the King of Mercia to thwart his uncle's ambitions. The millennium dawned darkly for Welsh hopes for better things. In the first 30 years of the new century new leaders did arise in Wales, who were new men, who owed nothing to distinguished ancestry and had no failures to live down: men like Rhydderch ap Iestyn, who ruled Deheubarth from 1023 to 1033, and Aeddan ap Blegywryd, lord of Gwynedd until 1018 and above all, Llywelyn ap Seisyll, who held sway in Gwynedd until he too met a violent death in 1023. However, it was this new man's son, Gruffudd ap Llywelyn, who, in the middle years of the eleventh century, was to transform the history of the Welsh people, to whom for a few brief years he offered a bright dream of freedom..

Before describing how Gruffudd ap Llywelyn rose above all his difficulties to become the King of Wales, a short diversion is necessary in order to allow the reader to realise that before the tenth century ended there was as much change and confusion east of Offa's Dyke as there was west of it. The rightly-called Golden Age of the Saxon Monarchy came to an end with the death of Edgar the Peaceful in 975; he was the last Saxon king to enjoy the homage of all the rulers of Wales and the north of England. The story of this

King Edgar being rowed up the river Dee at Chester by six kings may not be strictly true, but it has at least allegorical value. The next five years witnessed a succession of weak rulers in England, which gave the Vikings (the Danes) the opportunity they sought. From 980 the floodgates were forced as once more Danish invaders poured into eastern England, bringing years of fear and uncertainty that were to last until 1016.

Three years previously, in 1013, a Viking chief with a formidable name and temper to match, Sweyn Forkbeard, seized the throne. He was succeeded in 1016 by his son, Canute, who was to prove a wise and successful ruler, whose reign from 1016 to 1035 provided his people with much-needed years of peace, which at his death gave way to a return to lawlessness and in-fighting.

It was in this period of uncertainty that a strong man came to the fore: Godwin, the Saxon Earl of Hereford. In 1042, when the Danish line of kings came to an end with the death of Hardicanute, Godwin, who cherished a secret ambition one day to establish a dynasty, filled the vacant throne of England by inviting over from Normandy Edward, whose Saxon father,

Ethelred the Unready had lived there in exile. This new king, Edward the Confessor, though a Saxon, had a Norman mother, by whom he had been educated in Norman ways. Godwin had made him king partly to offset the rapidly-rising power of ruler of Mercia and partly because he knew that the saintly and cultured Edward would be able to do nothing to stop him from becoming the power behind the throne. When Godwin died in 1051, his son Harold succeeded to the earldom and to the position of great authority enjoyed by his father; this Harold, too, had ambitions – and in addition, the qualities that would enable him to realise them. Within a decade his path would cross that of Gruffudd ap Llywelyn.

The actual date of Gruffudd's birth is unknown, but he was probably well into his thirties before he had his chance; his father, Llywelyn ap Seisyll had seized power in Gwynedd and Powys in 1018. His reign lasted for only five years, but they were years of strong and successful government. This came to a sudden end when he was murdered by his own men in 1023. He was succeeded by Iago ap Idwal, who ruled Gwynedd and Powys until 1039, when his men turned on him too and killed him, giving Gruffudd his chance to step into his father's footsteps. It is an unfortunate but significant fact of Welsh history that again and again Welshmen eased the path of conquest for their country's enemies by killing their fellow Welshmen.

History provided many an example of princes who, in their green and youthful years, showed little interest in anything beyond the sowing of wild oats; so it was with Gruffudd ap Llywelyn. Chroniclers refer to his indolence in youth, his refusal to accept any responsibility; these same chroniclers also noted the sudden change that came over him once the responsibility of kingship had been thrust upon him, in 1039. He quickly revealed unsuspected qualities of imaginative leadership; he was brave and far-sighted, energetic and steadfast. Wales indeed has produced few leaders of his calibre and yet, as will be seen, it all seemed to turn to dust, as he too eventually died at the hands of fellow-Welshmen.

Hardly had his reign started than he chose to clash with his Mercian neighbours in the east, forcing them to do battle with him near the river Severn at Rhyd-y-Groes, close to Welshpool. He gained a notable victory, putting the Mercians to flight. By this daring and decisive assault Gruffudd made the Marches safe from further attack for the time being, thus enabling him to turn his full attention to his main objective, which was to conquer Deheubarth, whose ruler at this time was Hywel ap Edwin. This task was to occupy Gruffudd on and off for 16 years.

Deheubarth, the third of the major provinces of Wales at this time, was ruled by Hywel ap Edwin, who had no intention of playing second fiddle to Gruffudd. There is a dearth of detailed information about the numerous bloody encounters between these two men, so that little more than an outline of their activities is now possible. In the first two years of his reign Gruffudd, in addition to his excursion into Mercia, twice attacked Ceredigion, in the course of the second attack setting fire to Llanbadarn Fawr (today an eastern suburb of Aberystwyth). The following year Hywel again tasted defeat at the battle of Pencader, but though beaten in battle, Hywel still had sufficient forces to deprive Gruffudd of his prey. In 1044, however, Gruffudd seemed likely to gain control of Deheubarth when he not only defeated

Hywel but also killed him in a tussle near Cardigan. Still, however, Deheubarth refused to yield, finding itself a new champion in Gruffudd ap Rhydderch, who in his bid to establish himself in authority cajoled the assistance of Swegen, a younger son of the Saxon Earl of Hereford, Godwin. For some years Gruffudd ap Rhydderch managed to defy Gruffudd ap Llywelyn, who had to content himself with occasional forays into the Cardiganshire countryside. Finally in 1055 Gruffudd, the Gwynedd one, freed for a while from other commitments, defeated and killed Gruffudd ap Rhydderch in battle and went on at long last to annex Deheubarth. Shortly afterwards he succeeded in adding to his conquests both Morgannwg and Gwent. In 1055, Gruffudd ap Llywelyn was indeed the 'King of All Wales', becoming the first Welshman ever to enjoy authority over the whole of his country.

By this time, in the east of Britain Harold's star was in the ascendant; he had taken over responsibility from his father, Godwin in 1051 and had soon involved himself in the affairs of the Marches, where the Mercian leader Aelfgar was defying his authority. Gruffudd, realising that the Marches were in a ferment, had in 1052 stayed his hand for a while from attacking Deheubarth to lead an army across Offa's Dyke, where he gained the better of an English army in a battle near Leominster. After disposing of his Welsh enemies in the south and south-west, Gruffudd in 1056 felt strong enough to move east again; he had been shrewd enough to make a friend of Harold's enemy, the ruler of Mercia, and with this leader Aelfgar at his side he attacked Hereford, drove out the defending army and set fire to the cathedral, before withdrawing to the hills in the west. Soon the English regrouped themselves, and in June 1056 again faced Gruffudd and Aelfgar in battle. Again Gruffudd and his Mercian ally gained the mastery, but the outcome of the campaign was surprising because in the ensuing discussions Gruffudd, probably sensing the danger of over-reaching himself, agreed to return to Wales and surprisingly promised thereafter to pay homage to Edward the Confessor.

This unusual alliance between Wales and Mercia was further strengthened by the marriage of Gruffudd to Aelfgar's daughter, Ealdgyth; in consequence Gruffudd hoped in future to enjoy increased security on his eastern borders. This hope was to clash with the ambitions of Harold, who took advantage of the later weakening of the alliance, when Aelfgar died. In 1061, Harold established himself in the south of Gwent, from where he was systematically to move northwards, getting ever nearer to reaching his goal: to challenge Gruffudd ap Llywelyn. The great clash between Celt and Saxon was about to begin.

Between 1061 and 1063, Harold engaged in many skirmishes with the Welsh and he slowly but methodically confirmed his position in the southern Marches. Giraldus Cambrensis, who wrote little more than a century after the events he described, paid tribute to the thorough preparations he made for his campaign. He also wrote: 'in commemoration of his successes ... a great number of inscribed stones [were] put up in Wales to mark the many places where he won a victory. This was the old custom. The stones bear the inscription *HIC FUIT VICTOR HARALDUS*'. ['Here Harold was victorious'.] The modern editor in a footnote explains that no such stones have survived. Curious readers who live in Gwent may care to muse upon a sun-dial, which had in modern times been taken into the church at Trelech; this dial has carved upon it a local Bronze Age alignment, a Norman motte and a medieval wall. Engraved on the top are the words *HIC FUIT VICTOR HARALDUS*. The accompanying date 1689 prompts the thought that such a victory stone as that described by Giraldus Cambrensis was still to be seen locally in the late seventeenth century, when the stone-mason copied the words. Further evidence, linking Harold with this area of Gwent is furnished by the Bronze Age standing stones, also at Trelech, which bear the anachronistic name of Harold's Stones!

Harold, after extending and consolidating his hold on Gwent and Powys, in 1062 marched into north Wales in an attempt to settle with his archenemy Gruffudd; by the next year he was ready for the battle, which resulted in Gruffudd being driven out of his palace at Rhuddlan. Harold took his time, first destroying the palace before moving further into north Wales in pursuit of the retreating Gruffudd, who took refuge in Snowdonia. Again, according to Giraldus Cambrensis, Harold organised his campaign brilliantly, making sure of his food supply in Anglesey

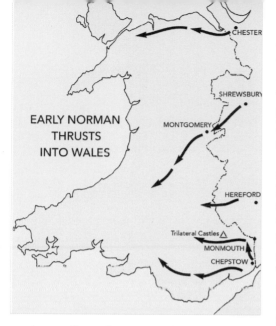

EARLY NORMAN THRUSTS INTO WALES

when Edward the Confessor died. Later that same year the last Saxon King of England himself died at Hastings, whose victor was before long to mount a far greater threat to the Welsh than any they had known before. Dark days indeed lay ahead for Wales.

All was by no means lost, however. Gruffudd ap Llywelyn, humbled and humiliated, had yet served his country well; not only had he succeeded in uniting Wales politically, he had also instilled into his fellow-countrymen a national spirit, a determination to resist. This was to stand Wales in good stead in the troubled years after the Normans, having captured England and broken the Saxons in a matter of months, turned westwards to bring about what they expected to be an easy and speedy conclusion to their island conquest.

Early Norman Infiltration

From prehistoric times to the eleventh century Wales was repeatedly overrun; men of the New Stone Age, the Bronze Age and the Iron Age fought and killed, intermarried and settled down for a while, eventually to be followed by the Romans in the first century AD, who for the most

by sending a fleet to stand off the coast of north Wales. The end was an anticlimax, no final battle being necessary, as once again Welshmen turned upon their own and killed Gruffudd. They completed their act of treachery by sending his head to Saxon Harold.

For the first time, the hated Saxons seemed to have gained the mastery over the Welsh. Harold, however, soon had other business to attend to. In January 1066, he seized the throne of England,

part occupied parts of Wales only in a military sense. At the beginning of the fifth century, when the Roman legions received their marching orders, new invaders promptly arrived from Strathclyde, Cunedda and his men, who came and saw and conquered before proceeding to provide a large part of Wales with strong government for many centuries. Eastern Wales in the seventh century began to feel the might of the new Saxon occupiers of what is now England; these fierce Saxons, whether they came from Northumbria, Mercia or Wessex, made life miserable for eastern areas of Wales on and off for 400 years, until, as was related previously, they defeated Gruffudd ap Llywelyn. This Saxon triumph was to prove a hollow one, because only three years later the Saxon hold on England itself was ended by the victory at Hastings of new invaders from France, the Christianized Vikings whom historians call Normans. 1066 is not seen as a significant date in the annals of Wales; nevertheless, with the benefit of hindsight, Wales too should probably regard 1066 as

Early key Norman castles in their attempt to conquer Wales: 1. Chester; 2. Shrewsbury; 3. Chepstow

something of a landmark, because thereafter the danger to them from their eastern neighbours achieved a much greater intensity than ever before. Whatever the method chosen by the new rulers in London, whether infiltration or delegation of power by the king to feudal vassals, strategically placed, or outright military assault, the threat to Welsh hopes of independence became far more menacing after 1066.

It is a matter of debate as to when it is correct to drop the use of the word Norman in favour of the word English, but in the context of this book an arbitrary dividing line has been chosen, that of 1189, when King Henry II died. By Norman infiltration is meant the various methods and policies by means of which the victors over the English at Hastings sought to spread their dominion westwards beyond Offa's Dyke. It should also be borne in mind that during these early years of Norman infiltration into Wales, the defeated Saxons, back in England, were also feeling the full force of their new repressive Norman masters. In one afternoon the Saxons were crushed under the Norman heel, to all intents and purposes, and any rebellions soon waned as the old English ruling gentry were wiped out. For the first century and a half after the battle of Hastings the Normans were the complete masters of England, and the Saxons were relegated to the role of obedient or recalcitrant providers of labour for their unloved masters. Saxon peasants tended the herds of cows and flocks of sheep, which, when served at table to their Norman overlords, became beef and mutton; cow and sheep belonged to the language of the defeated Saxons, while beef and mutton, which only the visitors were supposed to eat, were words which the Norman invaders had brought with them from France. French became the language of power and law in England.

As France was the most developed feudal country in Europe, it was natural that, when Norman William left France for England, he brought his feudal ideas with him; he found a certain amount of local feudalism already in existence in England, which he quickly developed and centralised. As supreme overlord he infeudated important fiefs to his Norman henchmen, three of whom were appointed for the express purpose of concerning themselves with the conquest of Wales. It has to be stressed that these vassals, apart from their periodic appearance at court, tended to act independently of their overlords; evidence of this was to be forthcoming in the early days of Norman infiltration in Wales, when the Marcher lords frequently acted without reference to London. Apart from an expedition into the south-western part of Wales in 1081, kings of England seemed to take little personal part in developments in Wales until Henry I became king in 1100.

Once England was pacified, William I turned his attention to the conquest of Wales; first, in 1067, he infeudated his cousin, William Fitzosbern, to whom he gave the lapsed title of the Earl of Hereford (formerly owned by the Saxon Harold). Next, in 1070, he made Roger Montgomery Earl of Shrewsbury and Hugh of Avranches Earl of Chester. These three Norman vassals were virtually given plenipotentiary powers to plan and execute the conquest of Wales, as they separately saw fit. They had not anticipated, however, that a fierce 200-year struggle was awaiting them.

The king's cousin, Fitzosbern, Earl of Hereford, wasted no time in carrying out his master's instructions; above all he had a good eye for choosing the right places for setting up his strong points. Today's visitor is recommended to visit Chepstow, where on a cliff above the river Wye, where it enters the sea, the first Norman castle to be built in Wales may still be seen. Much has been added since, of course, but the Great Tower remains to pay tribute to Fitzosbern's choice of site. Most early Norman castles consisted of wooden towers, erected on top of mounds of earth and surrounded by wooden palisades and a moat. Not so this one at Chepstow (*Striguil*), which was made of stone, thereby indicating the importance attached to it for mounting an attack on the Wye valley.

Further north, Monmouth, less than 20 miles (32.18 km) above Chepstow, was also marked down by Fitzosbern as a suitable site for another castle, which in the event proved ideal both for attack and for defence. At Monmouth the two rivers Wye and Monnow join up, thus providing an excellent defensive position. Of Monmouth's massive Norman castle nothing now remains except a green mound, but even today one can get some idea of the castle's former size by remembering when standing in Agincourt Square in front of the Shire Hall that one is in fact in the very middle of what was once the castle's outer bailey. Once Monmouth's castle was finished, Fitzosbern looked about for outer defences and decided in order to complete the defences of this key town to build three more fortifications north of the town and west of the river Monnow. The three places chosen for this extra forward protection were Grosmont, Skenfrith and Whitecastle, which together became known as the Trilateral; today they are amongst Gwent's most attractive historical sites.

These early castles consisted of wooden keeps on top of earthen mounds, surrounded by wooden palisades beneath which were large enclosed areas where the soldiers had their huts and grew their food. These baileys, too, were protected by wooden fences and deep ditches, which were sometimes filled with water. They were very useful indeed in the short term to hold down an area and to provide reasonable security for the garrison, but in the course of time weather and fire took a heavy toll on them.

Meanwhile in the central region Roger Montgomery, the newly-created Earl of Shrewsbury, crossed Offa's Dyke and established himself 15 miles (24 km) south-west of Shrewsbury, where he built a castle, to which he gave his name, although the Welsh continued to know the place as Trefaldwyn. From here incursions into central Wales were planned and carried out by Roger. Montgomery today is a delightful small Georgian town, which no railway ever reached; it is a retreat for the connoisseur.

Further north, Hugh of Avranches set about organising a thrust into northern Wales; first he moved into Flintshire, where he empowered his deputy Robert to act in his name. Choosing a site by the river Clwyd, previously favoured by the late Gruffudd ap Llywelyn, Robert built a castle at Rhuddlan, whose name he then added to his own. Thereafter Robert of Rhuddlan moved with great speed along the coast, first stopping at the mouth of the river Conwy to build a castle at Deganwy, before penetrating as far as Caernarfon, which he likewise fortified (the massive castle of later days stands on the same site).

Returning to the south of the country, a descendant of Rhodri Mawr, Rhys ap Tewdwr (whom Giraldus Cambrensis was later to claim as his great grandfather) became the ruler of Deheubarth in 1075, the same Giraldus referring to him as the Prince of South Wales. Six years later, however, in 1081 he was driven out of his headquarters at Dinefwr Castle by a fellow Welshman, Caradog ap Gruffudd, but was soon reinstated with the help of Gruffudd ap Cynan, of whom much will be said later. Before long William I, at last sufficiently freed from domestic problems, made a personal reconnaissance into southern Wales, getting as far west as St David's. At an unknown location the king had a meeting with Rhys ap Tewdwr, as a result of which an agreement was reached which was to assure peace for Rhys ap Tewdwr for the remaining six years of William's life. Rhys was thus enabled to deal with the pressing problem of local Welsh resistance to his rule. It is perhaps worth noting that the price the ruler of Deheubarth had agreed to pay to the Normans was an annual sum of £40, and so Rhys ap Tewdwr found himself a vassal of the King of England, thus establishing an important precedent.

In 1088, the year after the death of

The Trilateral Norman castles in Gwent: 1. Grosmont; 2. Skenfrith; 3. Whitecastle

William I and the accession of William II, Rhys' authority in Deheubarth was undermined by a strong attack made by the ruler of Powys; initially the assault succeeded and for a short time Rhys had to flee to Ireland, from which refuge he soon returned, with very welcome Viking assistance, and decisively defeated the army of Powys and restored his authority in Deheubarth. Three years later yet another assault was mounted by Powys, which was firmly dealt with by Rhys at the battle of St Dogmaels. Powys had at long last been defeated but it had been so seriously weakened by its many military adventures that when the Normans attacked the province, under the aegis of the new king, William II, they were able quickly to overrun the central part of Powys. This attack Rhys did his best to contain but died in the attempt, meeting his end near Brecon in 1093. Soon Bernard de Newmarch managed to create a Norman fief around Brecon and another Norman thrust from the south; this one, under Philip de Braose, moved north to capture Radnor. There were other Norman successes at Longtown and Abergavenny, while Robert Fitzhamon crossed the Severn from Gloucester and defeated Iestyn, the ruler of Morgannwg, before setting up the lordship of Glamorgan. Further north in Powys members of Roger Montgomery's family penetrated to the west and south-west from their castle stronghold, overran Ceredigion and established new headquarters in Pembroke.

A return visit is now necessary to Gwynedd to follow the career of another remarkable descendant of Rhodri Mawr, Gruffudd ap Cynan, whose grandfather Iago, ruler of Gwynedd, had been murdered in 1039. The dead ruler's son Cynan had lived in exile in Ireland, where he married the daughter of one of the Viking ruling families in Dublin. Their twenty-year son Gruffudd in 1075 crossed over into Wales in the fond hope that he might win back for himself and his family the overlordship of Gwynedd. By this time the Norman Robert of Rhuddlan was actively trying to expand his authority further westwards, thus coming into conflict with the usurping ruler of Gwynedd, Trahaearn. The enterprising Gruffudd ap Cynan, surveying the political

Twthill - the site of the early Norman motte and bailey castle at Rhuddlan

scene, formed an alliance with Robert of Rhuddlan, who shared a common enemy, the *de facto* ruler of Gwynedd, whose delegated lieutenant in the Llŷn peninsula, Cynwrig, was killed in a battle with Gruffudd. Later that same year Gruffudd engaged the usurper Trahaearn in battle and gained the mastery, which enabled him to restore his family's fortunes by becoming the ruler of Gwynedd.

Gruffudd ap Cynan soon began to flex his muscles, daring to take the offensive against his former ally, Robert. He laid siege to Rhuddlan Castle, which he failed to capture, although he returned home with a considerable quantity of booty. Meanwhile, the defeated Trahaearn rallied his forces and attacked Gruffudd; this time he succeeded in turning the tables on him, forcing Gruffudd once more to take refuge in Ireland. In 1081, Gruffudd returned from Ireland, but with some necessary circumspection landed on the coast of Ceredigion, where he made common

cause with Rhys ap Tewdwr, whom he helped to rescue Deheubarth from Caradog ap Gruffudd. Rhys in gratitude then helped Gruffudd ap Cynan to regain his authority over Gwynedd in a battle in which Trahaearn was killed. Thus Gruffudd became ruler of Gwynedd for a second time, but not for long did he enjoy his newly-acquired authority, because the Normans soon tricked him into attending a peace conference near Corwen, turned on him and took him off to Chester, where he languished in a Norman prison for some years. The Normans then took advantage of his absence to extend their authority in Gwynedd, building strong points at Bangor, Caernarfon and at Beaumaris. Quite how long Gruffudd ap Cynan's captivity lasted is far from clear, but he had escaped and was a free man in 1094, because in that year he led a revolt against Norman rule in Gwynedd; in 1098 the Normans launched a two-pronged counter-offensive in northern Wales from Chester and Shrewsbury, which succeeded in driving Gruffudd into Anglesey, from where he soon found it necessary to flee to Ireland. The following year he was back in Anglesey in a position of authority, but only by grace and favour of the Normans, who soon allowed him back on to the mainland where he once again ruled Gwynedd.

Change was in the air; in 1100 William II died and Henry I, who succeeded him, made peace with Gruffudd ap Cynan, who for some years thereafter managed to rule in peace, bringing back a measure of prosperity and security to Gwynedd, in addition to throwing out its boundaries to include the lands between the Conwy and the Dee. By 1115 Henry I was ready to reawaken Norman ambitions in Wales, but as far as Gwynedd was concerned Gruffudd ap Cynan seems to have trodden very warily; he was by this time an old man, who had learned the hard way how best to handle the Normans. At any rate, without any overt loss of face or of authority he succeeded in keeping Henry's army out of Gwynedd. The two leaders were to die within two years of each other, Henry I in 1135 and Gruffudd in 1137. At the end Gruffudd was blind and maybe decrepit, but he had done a great deal to stiffen Gwynedd's resolve in any future collisions with the Normans.

When thinking about Wales at this time it is perhaps too easy to convey an oversimplified and therefore inaccurate impression of sturdy freedom-loving Welshmen bravely defending their lands against the ruthless ravages of the ever-encroaching Normans. That Welshmen defended stoutly and that the Normans consistently encroached cannot of course be gainsaid. But two caveats seem necessary. The first concerns the inability of the Welsh to agree amongst themselves, which would have enabled them to put a stronger, more united, front against the invader. Evidence of this lack of unity has been seen in the events recently described in the second half of the eleventh century, when Rhys ap Tewdwr clashed with Caradog ap Gruffudd and Gruffudd ap Cynan fought it out with Trahaearn.

The second caveat seems necessary when thought is given to the social organisation of the Welsh lands in Norman-occupied areas. The Norman advance was a piecemeal affair; after making initial capture of Welsh positions, the thorough Normans paused to consolidate. This they did by building mottes and baileys, from which they were able to exercise complete authority, civil as well as military, over a fairly-limited locality; in this social setting, where security was safeguarded by the presence of Norman soldiery in their mottes and baileys, towns of a sort grew up, most of whose original inhabitants are likely to have been Norman civilian settlers. Beyond the limited aegis of this Norman military and civil settlement, the majority of the Welsh population of the district still continued to live their separate lives, as far as possible unaffected by the activities of the occupying power. Hence it was that two more or less separate communities grew up, one Norman and one Welsh.

Notes and Illustrations

Eliseg's Pillar

This most important link with the times of Rhodri Mawr may still be seen near the ruins of the *Valle Crucis* monastery in a field, 2 miles (3.2 km) north of Llangollen (GR 203 445). It was erected by an uncle of Rhodri, Cyngen, the ruler of Powys, in honoured remembrance of the achievements of his great-grandfather, who had successfully stood out against the mighty Mercian, Offa. This pillar was probably the first free-standing monument of its kind in Wales; originally it must have been very spectacular indeed, as it was twice its present height, the cross-piece and the lower part of the shaft having fallen victim to the destructive powers of man and the climate. During the Civil War in the seventeenth century Parliamentary soldiers pulled down the monument, which sympathetic hands re-erected as best they could 140 years later. In the twelfth century the Cistercian monks who built a monastery in the nearby valley had been so impressed by its magnificence that they called their monastery *Valle Crucis*.

Aberffraw, royal seat of kings

Readers of this book who live in northern Wales will, of course, need no introduction to Anglesey; they will already know that the island is a historical treasure house whose attractions, nevertheless, need to be highlighted for the benefit of other readers. It is a quite extraordinary area, where there is an unbroken succession of settlement from prehistoric times. More than 2500 years after the first burials took place at Bryn Celli Ddu, Celtic tribesmen from Scotland settled in the west of the island, their leader, Cunedda, establishing his government on the west coast at Aberffraw (GR 357 690).

Life has largely ebbed away from Aberffraw today, leaving behind a delightful village by the sea, where, in succession to the rulers of Gwynedd, now swoop roseate terns, and oystercatchers strut. It is indeed a place of pilgrimage for those with a sense of the past; at low tide the islanded and ancient church of St Cwyfan beckons, while up above, on the cliffs to the north of the village is a New Stone Age burial chamber, Barclodiad y Gawres, which is one of the best Neolithic sites in Britain.

Two miles (3.2 km) to the east of Aberffraw is the village of Llangadwaladr, named after Cunedda's grandson, Cadwaladr; here was the burial ground of the royal rulers of Gwynedd. Around the fifteenth-century church is a post-Reformation churchyard, beneath which lie the royal graves, the memorial stone of one of which survives; having been dug up in the churchyard, it was taken into the church, where it was built into the north wall of the chancel, its Latin message still clear. It commemorates a King of

1. Valle Crucis *Abbey*; 2. *Eliseg's Pillar*; 3. *The 'princes of Gwynedd' celebration at Aberffraw*

Gwynedd, Catamanus (Cadfan turned into Latin!); he is here proclaimed to have been 'the wisest and most famous of kings'. The presence of this most precious early Christian memorial stone by itself justifies a visit to this part of an enchanted island.

Hywel Dda Memorial Gardens, St Mary's Street, Whitland, SA34 0PY (*Stryd y Santes Fair, Hendy-gwyn ar Daf*)
The memorial to Hywel Dda and the legal system he helped to establish in Wales was designed by Peter Lord from Aberystwyth, and includes a Garden and an Interpretive Centre. In choosing a garden as the basis of his design the artist intended that it should provide a quiet and contemplative environment in which to explore the laws of Hywel Dda and through them, early medieval Welsh Society. This legal system was known for its wisdom and justice.

Offa's Dyke

Towards the end of the eighth century, Offa, the Saxon King of Mercia, organised the throwing up of the dyke, which became thereafter a rough and ready boundary between the Celts and the Saxons. The area traversed by the dyke, which ran from Prestatyn to Chepstow, for many centuries

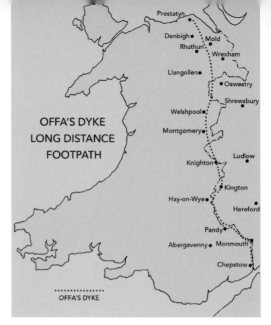

provided a meeting ground for the clash of cultures. Celtic to the west of it, Saxon and later Norman to the east. Today, happily, the tide of human conflict has left these still and beautiful hills but, as always, when the tide ebbs, much evidence of the former flooding remains, to which ruined castles, monasteries, green mounds and significant gaps in the dyke bear witness.

Of the original dyke only about 80 miles (129 km) of actual bank and ditch survive, but thanks to the skill and persistence of a band of devoted Welsh and English enthusiasts, who knew their history and loved the countryside, advantage was taken of the provisions of the National Parks Act, and a Long Distance Footpath was created from Prestatyn to Chepstow. The accompanying map will show the route taken by the path, which is 168 miles (270 km) long, and is thoroughly way-marked; it came into being in 1971 and includes 60 miles (96 km) of the original dyke. The maintenance of the path today is the voluntary responsibility of the Offa's Dyke Association, whose headquarters fittingly are in Knighton (Powys), whose name in Welsh, Trefyclawdd, indicates its position on the Dyke. Readers (some of whom, it is hoped, will venture on to the Dyke) are recommended to visit the Association's offices in the Old Primary School in Knighton, which is also the home town of the late Frank Noble, the man who inspired the creation of the Long Distance Footpath, and whose name will always be most closely associated with it.

At the Offa's Dyke Heritage Centre, Knighton

The Knitting Together of Wales

National awakening under Owain Gwynedd and Rhys ap Gruffudd

The twelfth century began with the accession of Henry I to the throne of England; at this time, the Normans held in Wales all lands east of the river Conwy, most of central Powys, Pembrokeshire and Morgannwg. The outlook for Welsh hopes of independence looked bleak indeed, despite the successful efforts in the early years of the century of Gruffudd ap Cynan to consolidate his power west of the Conwy, and of Owain Cadwgan to strengthen his hold on Powys. However, as so often happened in the history of Wales, the emergency produced leaders of uncommon ability and sense: Gruffudd ap Cynan's son, Owain Gwynedd, and Rhys ap Gruffudd, grandson of the mighty Rhys ap Tewdwr.

Owain, born in 1100, did much in the 1120s to help his elder brother Cadwallon to share the responsibilities of governing Gwynedd, as their father Gruffudd ap Cynan was now advanced in years. In addition the two brothers extended the authority of Gwynedd into new parts of Meirionnydd. Cadwallon died in 1132, five years before his father, leaving Owain as the potential successor to his father's dominions. In 1136, in alliance with Gruffudd ap Rhys in southern Wales, Owain completely defeated an army of Normans at Crug Mawr near Cardigan, the result of which was that no further Norman armies penetrated Deheubarth for the following 40 years. The next year, 1137, saw the death not only of Gruffudd ap Cynan but also of Gruffudd ap Rhys, whose youngest son Rhys, at that time but four years old, would one day become like Owain, an outstanding leader. Nevertheless, the deaths in the same year of Gruffudd ap Cynan and Gruffudd ap Rhys, staunchest of upholders of Welsh rights against Norman encroachment, would have meant a very serious threat indeed to Welsh hopes of holding the Normans at bay, but for the fortuitous coincidence of an acute political crisis in England, where the death of Henry I at the end of 1135 had been followed by a succession crisis. As Henry's only son had predeceased him, the succession should have gone by rights to his daughter Matilda, but there were many who doubted the ability of a woman to cope with the manifold difficulties of that time. Civil war ensued, as a result of which the new king was Stephen, grandson of William I.

This unlooked-for piece of good fortune prompted the Welsh to rise in a revolt, led by Anarawd and Cadell, elder sons of the late Gruffudd ap Rhys. Stephen's troubled reign lasted until 1154. During those years not only did the Welsh revolt flourish (Rhys ap Gruffudd in 1146, at the tender age of 13 years, fought his first battle against the Normans at the side of his older brother Maredudd, under the leadership of Cadell), but in Gwynedd Owain, who had succeeded in 1137, took full advantage of the divisions in English society to greatly strengthen the power of Gwynedd. By 1152, not only had he annexed much territory east of the Conwy, but his co-princes in Powys and Deheubarth had won back lands previously under Norman control. If fate seemed to have smiled on the Welsh in 1135, it certainly frowned upon them in 1154, when Stephen's death brought to the throne of England the rejected Matilda's son, who became Henry II; Henry soon gave every sign that he intended to be master in his own house. In the very next year Rhys ap Gruffudd succeeded his brother Maredudd as ruler of Deheubarth; thereafter Rhys ap Gruffudd was to join Owain Gwynedd in providing strong leadership and stern opposition to Henry's ambitious plan for a speedy conquest of Wales.

As Henry II was a vigorous and forthright young king with firm views about the future of Wales, a further extension of the Norman-Welsh conflict was inevitable, although at the start of his reign he was for a while much preoccupied with events in France, which demanded the presence in that country of many of his most-seasoned troops. In 1157, however, Henry found the time to make a sudden descent upon northern Wales, managing to deprive Owain Gwynedd of his recent conquest and forcing him to recall from exile his young brother, Cadwaladr, whom Owain had exiled five years previously. Furthermore Owain was also compelled to hand over to his brother a share in the government of Gwynedd and to pay homage to the king. In the same year Henry also forced his other main enemy in Wales, Rhys ap Gruffudd to bow the knee and to render homage, at the same time evacuating the recently-captured Ceredigion.

Henry possessed immense energy and the strongest of nerves; for, in addition to probing Welsh defences and trying to anticipate every Welsh move, he had a bitter constitutional quarrel on his hands in England, between himself and the Church of England. The Archbishop of Canterbury, Thomas Becket, proved an implacable enemy to the power of the throne throughout the 1160s. By 1163 Owain Gwynedd and Rhys ap Gruffudd, uncle and nephew, had come to a clear understanding how best to handle a difficult situation, the elder for the time being advising caution to the younger. Hence in 1163 Rhys ap Gruffudd, having been tricked away from Wales to the Norman court at Woodstock, listened to Owain's advice and meekly swore allegiance to the king, who, apparently satisfied with this declaration of loyalty, allowed him to return to Dinefwr Castle. There Rhys quickly recovered his nerve, as he planned the next move.

1164 saw the outbreak of a general revolt in Wales against Norman power, as Owain and Rhys realised that the quarrel between Henry II and his Archbishop was becoming increasingly serious. Owain Gwynedd soon succeeded in winning back some of his lost territory in the north, while in the south Rhys ap Gruffudd seized Ceredigion. Henry, it must be remembered, in addition to his domestic problems in England, had many calls on his time in France, most of which country he had ruled even before becoming King of England; indeed Henry II was the most powerful ruler in Europe, save only for the Holy Roman Emperor himself, the mighty Barbarossa. Early in 1165, when circumstances conspired to make it possible for Henry to turn aside for a while from the problems of France and the constitutional quarrel in England with the Church, he decided to deal (he hoped, effectively and finally) with the troublesome Welsh. In July there assembled in Shrewsbury and Oswestry the largest army ever committed to the conquest of Wales; in its ranks served the finest fighters of France as well as the flower of the Norman army. Meanwhile the defenders of Wales, faced with a common danger, for once agreed to act in unison, with substantial military detachments from Deheubarth and Powys

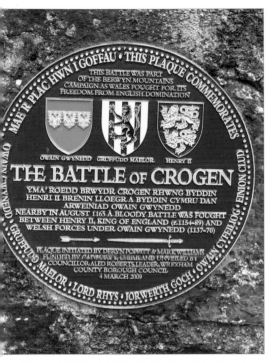

THIS PLAQUE COMMEMORATES • MAE'R PLAC HWN I GOFFÁU

THIS BATTLE WAS PART
OF THE BERWYN MOUNTAINS
CAMPAIGN AS WALES FOUGHT FOR ITS
FREEDOM FROM ENGLISH DOMINATION

OWAIN GWYNEDD GRUFFUDD MAELOR HENRI II

THE BATTLE OF CROGEN

YMA' ROEDD BRWYDR CROGEN RHWNG BYDDIN
HENRI II BRENIN LLOEGR A BYDDIN CYMRU DAN
ARWEINIAD OWAIN GWYNEDD
NEARBY IN AUGUST 1165 A BLOODY BATTLE WAS FOUGHT
BETWEEN HENRY II, KING OF ENGLAND (c.1154-89) AND
WELSH FORCES UNDER OWAIN GWYNEDD (1137-70)

PLAQUE INITIATED BY DERYN POPPITT & MARK WILLIAMS
FUNDED BY CADBURY'S CHILILAND UNVEILED BY
COUNCILLOR ALED ROBERTS, LEADER, WREXHAM
COUNTY BOROUGH COUNCIL
4 MARCH 2009

OWAIN GWYNEDD • GRUFFUDD MAELOR • LORD RHYS • IORWERTH GOCH • IONAF CYFELIOG • EINION CLUD

A reminder of the Battle of Crogen in the Ceiriog valley in 1165 when the united Welsh army under Owain Gwynedd halted the invasion of Henry II's huge ambitious forces

joining the forces of Gwynedd, drawn up in Corwen under the leadership of Owain Gwynedd with Rhys ap Gruffudd at his side.

In August, this great army of Henry II marched westwards up the Ceiriog valley towards the uninviting slopes of the Berwyn mountains, beyond which, in Corwen, stood waiting the combined armies of Wales. However, the ambitions of even the greatest soldiers, as Napoleon Bonaparte was to discover in a later century, had to yield in the face of the rigours of climate. Just as Generals January and February were to thwart French ambitions in Russia, so General August denied Henry's much-vaunted army even the sight of the main army of the Welsh. That August, as the invading army slowly trudged up on to the Berwyn mountains, the incessant rain and the buffeting wind, aided and abetted by the darting raids of Welsh guerilla bands, made life unbearable and progress impossible for Henry's army. The Welsh army in Corwen was not vouchsafed even a glimpse of the vanguard of the Normans as mud and the moorland bogs, sodden supplies, and the never-ceasing deluge of rain drove the Normans back into

England. Henry, it has to be said, vented his spleen on his hostages, 22 of whom were mutilated, including two sons of Owain Gwynedd.

In the remaining five years of Owain Gwynedd's life Henry II was far too concerned with happenings in Ireland, France and England to be able to pay much attention to what was going on in Wales, where Owain succeeded in pushing back Gwynedd's eastern boundaries, in the process destroying the castles of Basingwerk and Rhuddlan. Further south, however, in Powys, little progress was made on the Welsh side as internal jealousies once again took their toll, although in Deheubarth, Rhys ap Gruffudd went from strength to strength, adding new territories to his dominions. In 1170 the great Owain Gwynedd died, and was buried near the high altar in the cathedral at Bangor – despite the fact that he had been excommunicated by the Archbishop of Canterbury, Thomas Becket, who had regarded Owain's second marriage, to his cousin, as incestuous. Incestuous or not, Owain Gwynedd is rightly regarded as one of the great rulers of Wales, who in standing up so successfully to Norman attacks, set a fashion, which was successfully imitated by Rhys ap Gruffudd, Llywelyn ap Iorwerth and by Llywelyn ap Gruffudd.

With the death of Owain Gwynedd the leadership of the Welsh cause passed from northern Wales to the south, where Rhys ap Gruffudd was soon to become the most powerful man in the country. (Giraldus Cambrensis, their contemporary, it is interesting to note, always referred to Owain Gwynedd as the prince of northern Wales and to Rhys ap Gruffudd as the prince of southern Wales.) In the remaining years of Henry's reign (he died in 1189) circumstances so played into Rhys' hands that he rapidly achieved a position of great power and influence. Apart from the distraction of the quarrel with the Church, Henry was faced by an unexpected development in Ireland, where he was asked to intervene in a local rebellion. The troops detailed for service in Ireland were drawn from the Norman garrison in Pembrokeshire, whose presence south of Deheubarth had up to then exerted a restraining influence on the policies of Rhys ap Gruffudd. With the deterioration of the military position in Ireland making it necessary for Henry to go in person, the king took the opportunity to travel there via Pembrokeshire, where he summoned Rhys to his presence. A strangely friendly relationship developed between the men, which the king found it politically wise to cherish. Henry, before embarking for Ireland, paid a state visit to St David's, where he officially recognised Rhys as the ruler of Deheubarth, at the same time authorising him to retain all his recent conquests.

In 1172, on his return from Ireland, Henry again met Rhys, this time at Laugharne, where he appointed him Justiciar of South Wales, thereafter always referring to him as the Arglwydd Rhys (*Lord Rhys*). By this time the king must have decided that a firm understanding with Rhys was politically essential, as it would serve to offset the growing strength of some of Henry's overambitious Marcher lords. From then on Rhys ap Gruffudd ruled absolutely in southern Wales – and was frequently observed in the king's company in the royal court in England. Clearly the king and his Welsh Justiciar came to enjoy full confidence in each other.

Back in Wales, Rhys became ever more confident, as his reputation as the greatest living Welshman grew apace; at Dinefwr, his ancestral home, there was much enlarging of the ancient castle, while the addition of Ceredigion and other lands in the far west made it desirable for Rhys to move his headquarters to Cardigan, where another stout fortress was built. Here in 1176 a great eisteddfod took place, to which competitors were invited from far and wide. The poetry chair was won by a man of Gwynedd, while the prize for music was awarded to one of Rhys' own men. As well as being a patron of the arts, he also concerned himself with spiritual matters, lending his patronage to the religious orders; indeed in 1184 he granted a charter for the foundation of a Cistercian monastery at *Strata Florida*, of which more will be said in a later section. Most remarkably of all, perhaps, a successful and powerful Welsh prince was for the first time seen to be cooperating with a Norman King of England and openly assimilating, adopting the dress and the manners associated with the Normans.

In 1187, when the news of the Saracen recapture of Jerusalem reached Europe, there was an angry outcry and an immediate call for another crusade to rescue the Holy Places from the infidel. In

England, this call for another crusade was answered by the Archbishop of Canterbury, Baldwin, who had succeeded the ill-fated Becket. The Archbishop decided to conduct a recruiting pilgrimage around Wales, taking with him as his second-in-command, his interpreter and his advisor, a canon of St David's, Giraldus Cambrensis, who was a kinsman of Rhys ap Gruffudd. Rhys indeed met him a number of times during this famous journey through Wales in 1188, on one occasion entertaining him at Cardigan castle, where Rhys intended himself to volunteer for the crusade until he was talked out of it by his wife, Gwenllian.

In the next year Henry II died, before he could achieve his ambition to participate in the Third Crusade; this opportunity fell to his son, Richard I, the Lionheart, who was to become the Crusader Extraordinary. Richard's achievements as a crusader are well known, but as he spent only seven months of his ten-year reign in England, little can be said about his achievements as king. As far as Rhys ap Gruffudd was concerned, he very soon discovered that the prestigious days of royal cooperation were over; he reacted to royal indifference by taking the military offensive. He attacked and captured the Norman-held castles of Laugharne and Llansteffan, he ravaged Pembrokeshire and he laid unsuccessful siege to Carmarthen. His latter years were blighted by incessant family quarrels; of his eight sons, two actually fought against their father in battle, subsequently imprisoning him for a while, while two other sons were themselves imprisoned by Rhys for conspiring against him. After bringing an end to this bitter chapter of family feuding, Rhys spent the last two years of his life in once again taking up arms (and successfully too) against Norman Marcher lords in Powys; he died in 1197, his reputation shining brightly in the Welsh hall of fame, as he was certainly the greatest champion of Welsh independence south Wales ever produced. He probably died in the firm belief that Wales would continue to enjoy the privileges and the power which he and his uncle, Owain Gwynedd, had wrested from the Normans.

The Christian Church
in Medieval Wales

In Wales, as elsewhere in the British Isles, religion in the Middle Ages played a prominent part in everyday life; it has been said, and with some truth, that the two most popular occupations in those years were praying and fighting, which might prompt a cynic to observe that the combination of those two activities accounted for the popularity of the Crusades! Be that as it may, it seems desirable here to interrupt the chronological account of Welsh history in order to consider how the pattern of Christian development in Wales in earlier centuries had differed substantially from the pattern of development in England, and to show the importance of this deviation.

Christianity had originally reached Britain during the Roman occupation, becoming the official religion here in 314, when the Roman Emperor Constantine became a Christian. However, Christianity failed to survive in Britain when the Roman legions had to leave these shores early in the fifth century.

Later in that same century, Christian missionaries from Brittany brought Christianity back to the western part of Britain and proceeded to Christianise a great deal of what is now Wales, whereas Christianity only returned to eastern Britain, that is to say England, in the late sixth century, when Augustine came on a direct mission from Rome. Therefore long before Augustine began to rechristianise Kent and Northumbria, the Christian church had become firmly established in the far west.

In 602 Augustine, learning of the existence of a separate Christian church in the west, called its leaders to a conference, where the gap between the two churches, some of whose rituals and observances differed, was by no means bridged. In the following centuries the two churches in fact drew further apart, as they went their separate ways.

This was the state of affairs when the Normans appeared on the scene. The forebears of these Normans in the century before their conquest of England were Vikings, who had settled on the north coast of France, where they had soon embraced Christianity. Hence, when, after the conquest of Saxon England, they began to secure a foothold in Wales, they tried to make the Welsh churches conform to their own practices, in many cases even altering the very dedications of the churches. Existing Welsh churches, of course, had been dedicated to Celtic saints, like Dewi

(*St David*), Teilo, Beuno and Illtud, which thereafter had to yield place to Roman saints, most popular of whom was St Mary. A great many of today's villages called Llanfair (Mair – mutated into 'Fair' – is Welsh for Mary) began life with Celtic dedications. Gradually the authority of Canterbury grew in Wales, despite stubborn local opposition; senior Norman clerics were appointed as bishops, who, where necessary, created new dioceses into which existing parishes were made to fit. By the end of the twelfth century this process was still at work.

However, in those parts of Wales, where the Norman writ did *not* run, the ancient Celtic church retained its original character, many examples of which, set in their circular churchyards, still survive to uplift the spirits of those who delight in historical continuity. In the Celtic heartland as early as in the sixth century a simple monastic movement, which owed nothing to outside influences, developed here and there in various parts of Wales. It was a sensible pragmatic development, which generally followed in the wake of successful missionary activity. A number of Celtic missionaries, having set up their *llannau*, joined forces in a geographically central place, where a *clas* (monastery) was then established. These *clasau* became in many instances not only missionary headquarters for outlying *llannau*, but also centres of learning and culture, usually presided over by an abbott, such as those, among many others, at Llanilltud Fawr (Glamorgan), Llanddew, Glascwm and Meifod (Powys), at Clynnog Fawr (Gwynedd) and Llanynys (Clwyd). No *clas* survives today, partly because of the erosion of the years but more particularly because the Normans deliberately chose to break up the *clasau*. But, if in one respect by so doing the Normans set a pattern for Henry VIII, 500 years later, to imitate by seizing all the lands, the property and the endowments, in another respect the Normans did at least have something worthwhile to put in the place of the *clasau*.

Another monastic movement, very different from the earlier Welsh *clas*, had been growing in western Europe for several centuries before the Normans set foot in England; by Alfred's time it had achieved something of a settled existence in Saxon England, where the Benedictines had attracted many followers. After 1066, the Normans did all they could to encourage its development in England, where in the first years after the Norman conquest the Benedictines benefited most from Norman patronage, priories at Usk, Brecon and Ewenny furnishing evidence of Benedictine settlement in Wales. The enthusiasm generated a century later for the Third Crusade, which did much to account for the rapid expansion of monastic orders all over western Europe, found particular expression in the establishment of Cistercian monasteries in England and Wales; throughout the twelfth century the Cistercian order dominated the religious life of western Europe.

In Wales, which made a particular appeal to the Cistercians because of the wide choice of suitable sites in remote rural areas, their monks revealed a special skill in site selection and became expert in country crafts, of which sheep breeding was by far the most important. These Cistercian monks were plain and practical Christians who made a significant contribution to increasing the wealth of the districts where they settled. It has also to be said that while other monastic houses were established in Wales, more particularly the Benedictines and the Augustinians, their Welsh hosts rightly or wrongly tended to associate them with their Norman overlords. The Cistercians, though, in the course of time absorbed Welsh culture and Welsh customs and helped to build a bridge between those who cherished the ancient Celtic church and those who followed contemporary Christian practices.

The Cistercians must be saluted for doing so much to improve the economic life of Wales; not only did they practise and teach sheep-breeding skills, they also worked the silver and lead mines, they smelted the ore and they built the necessary bridges and roads to facilitate the transport of goods to market. In addition to their economic achievements the Welsh Cistercians were also noted scholars and patrons of the arts. In all, they established 15 monasteries in Wales, of which the first was at Neath and the second at Tintern (which will be described elsewhere in this book, where details will be provided of some of the visually exciting monasteries that have survived). Suffice it here to say that of the 15 Cistercian houses set up, probably the best-known are Tintern and *Strata Florida*, along with Benedictine monasteries and

Augustinian priories, of which the most outstanding is the one at Llanthony in Gwent.

Giraldus Cambrensis – Prelate and Chronicler

Towards the end of the twelfth century, in which the Welsh, as has already been seen, frequently oscillated between hope and despair, there came to his prime a man about whom more is known than about anyone else in Wales at any time in the Middle Ages. Giraldus Cambrensis, Gerald the Welshman, is unique in the contribution he makes to our understanding of people and places in twelfth-century Wales. Not only did he live at a supremely important stage in the struggle between England and Wales, but by virtue of his social rank, his position in the social hierarchy and his achievement in translating what he saw and what he thought about the issues of his time into words, which have come down to us, he was an outstanding source of information and informed comment. In all he wrote 17 books of which two in particular threw a searchlight on the Wales of his day.

His home was the castle at Manorbier on the Pembrokeshire coast a few miles west of Tenby; readers familiar with the district will already have decided that Gerald started life with immense advantages. The castle, which still stands, though within its walls a modern house has been discreetly and unobtrusively built, dominates one side of a sheltered bay, on the other side of which is St James' church, which alone would make worthwhile a visit to this delectable little seaside resort. Gerald was a man of many parts: as well as being a great student of all political and religious issues, he interested himself in a host of other things, customs and superstitions, strange facts of natural history, even in birdwatching, (although according to the expert opinion of William Condry he probably mistook a green woodpecker for a golden oriole!). All in all, had Gerald lived 300 years later he would probably have been acclaimed as a real man of the Renaissance.

In one respect Gerald was unique among those of his contemporaries, who commented on the passing scene; for, he

1. Gerallt Gymro – Gerald of Wales' statue at the City Hall, Cardiff; Norman abbeys in Wales: 2. Llanthony; 3. Neath; 4. Tintern

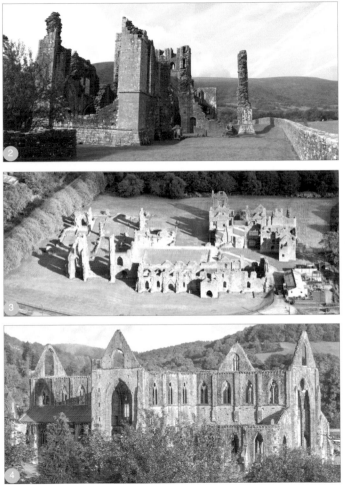

was of mixed lineage, part Norman and part Welsh. He was fortunate in so far as his Welsh kinsman Rhys ap Gruffudd, the Lord Rhys had already in the 1170s and 1180s, by his pragmatic change of policy, cooperated with the Normans when Henry II was king. He always referred to himself as a Welshman, though in fact he had more Norman than Welsh blood in his veins. When he was a boy in Manorbier on one occasion, when his parents were away from home, an attack, which was made on Tenby, was thought to endanger Manorbier; he quickly crossed over the valley and sought sanctuary in the parish church. It is interesting to note that this attack was being made by the Welsh on this powerfully-defended section of a Norman-held coastline. His father, in charge of Manorbier, was William de Barry, member of a Norman family who had taken their name from one of their conquests on the coast near Cardiff. William had married Angharad, the daughter of the Welsh princess Nest, who had married the Norman master of Pembroke Castle, Gerald of Windsor. This grandmother of Gerald the Welshman, Nest, was related to most of the royal princes of Wales; she was a woman of rare physical beauty, widely known as 'the Helen of Wales', but her morals were uncertain, as in addition to bearing five children to her husband, she bore five other children to different fathers, of whom the most famous was the Norman Henry I of England.

With his mixture of Norman and Welsh blood, Gerald was able to see the merits and demerits of both races, and was fair-minded enough to set them down in writing. It has also to be said that he regarded the English (the Saxons) with something approaching contempt. As he had two older brothers, Gerald was excused any responsibility for defending or maintaining the family possessions; from an early age he was marked out for a career in the church. His mother's brother was Bishop of St David's, who made himself responsible for his nephew's education. First he taught him Latin, and then, in 1156, when Gerald was ten, he sent him to the school that was attached to the Benedictine abbey in Gloucester. Here Gerald stayed for five years, excelling over all his peers so easily that at the age of 15 he was deemed ready for university. Paris, the most famous university in Europe at this time, was selected for this next stage of his education; here he spent ten years, in which his scholastic achievements were quite outstanding. In 1174, he returned home, well-equipped for a successful career in the church. With his ancestry and achievements, preferment was expected to be swift and splendid, and so it proved.

This distinguished graduate of the University of Paris, though not yet 30 years old, soon made his intention clear: it was to reform the church, to rid it of corruption, and to bring to book those who transgressed. Honours were heaped upon him, swift and fast. It was an age of pluralism and before long, still in 1174, this zealous, high-born would-be reformer received livings at Llanwnda, Mathri and Tenby in Pembrokeshire, as well as several others in England. In addition he was made a prebendary in Hereford and a canon at St David's. There were plenty of impoverished curates available to attend to all the parish duties involved, leaving Gerald free to attend to other matters, such as the non-payment of tithes in the diocese of St David's. Armed with the necessary evidence he journeyed to Canterbury and informed the Archbishop, who, suitably impressed by this display of zeal, made Gerald his personal representative and sent him back to Pembrokeshire with the necessary authority to enforce the payment. Next he investigated the theft of eight yoke of oxen from Pembroke Priory by none other than the Constable of Pembroke Castle, himself the Sheriff of the county, who in consequence was punished with excommunication. Next year, in 1175, Gerald visited Brecon, still vested with the authority of the Archbishop of Canterbury; there he called upon the local archdeacon, whose official residence was at Llanddew, a remote and hilly village to the north of Brecon. The elderly Archdeacon of Brecon, not expecting such a visit, was found to be keeping a mistress. Gerald reacted characteristically and suspended him then and there, whereupon the Archbishop of Canterbury, marvelling at his protegé's energy and success, ordered the Bishop of St David's (who, be it remembered, was Gerald's uncle and first tutor) to appoint his nephew Archdeacon of Brecon in place of the unfortunate old incumbent.

Gerald settled into his official residence in Llanddew, which was just across the road from the church, where there had been a *llan* since the sixth century. His house, the so-called Bishop's

Palace, has long since vanished, having been replaced by a succession of buildings on the same site, although Gerald's garden wall survives. His well continues to supply, now as then, the needs of the local community.

The new archdeacon set about his tasks in a fine fury of reforming zeal; he made a start by trying to improve the moral standards of the local priest, when he discovered that he was in the habit of sharing the revelling of his parishioners on patronal feasts, even, it was alleged, substituting cider for communion wine! Soon, when reports of clerical misdemeanours in Llanbadarn Fawr, near Llandrindod, reached his ears, he set forth to exact retribution. But news of his impending visit had already reached the parish; he was in consequence greeted by a shower of arrows, which caused the poor archdeacon to take shelter in the church, where for a while he had to undergo a siege.

In the following year, 1176, came a greater challenge; at Kerry, 3 miles (4.8 km) east of Newtown, the church had just been rebuilt and was therefore due for reconsecration. Two dioceses, St David's and St Asaph's, both claimed jurisdiction and therefore the right to reconsecrate St Michael's church. Gerald's famous uncle, the Bishop of St David's, alerted his nephew and told him to go there as quickly as possible and anticipate the arrival of the Bishop of St Asaph, who had already set out. Gerald reacted swiftly, reached Kerry, where he hurried through the churchyard and rushed into the church, where he at once ordered the bells to be rung to let the advancing bishop know that he was too late. The bishop however pressed on and soon joined the archdeacon in the church, where each cleric then proceeded to excommunicate the other! The people of Kerry, having interpreted the ringing of the bells on Gerald's orders as evidence that they were to be ruled by St David's turned upon the bishop and chased him out of the village.

These incidents all took place within 18 months of Gerald becoming archdeacon, but shortly afterwards, in 1176, Gerald's attention was diverted by an event of greater importance: his uncle died and the see of St David's became vacant. To become Bishop of St David's was certainly Gerald's ultimate goal, but not just for the

St David's Cathedral

gratification of personal vanity and ambition: had he succeeded in being appointed to this high office, he would have struggled with might and main to free the see of St David's from the jurisdiction of Canterbury, before going on to achieve full religious independence for the whole of Wales. On at least four occasions Gerallt was later offered Bishoprics, two in Ireland and two in Wales, all of which he refused because none of them would have given him the chance to cut religious ties with Canterbury. In 1176, the names of four candidates were submitted to Canterbury, including Gerald's; the decision was to be a joint one, from the

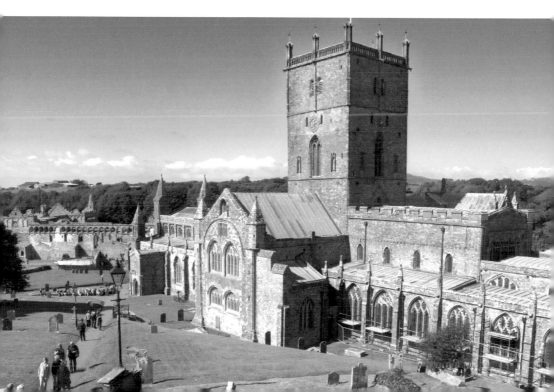

Archbishop and Henry II. The vacant see was filled by the Cluniac Prior of Much Wenlock, Peter de Leia.

The upshot was that Gerald at once left for France, leaving to one side his duties as Archdeacon of Brecon. He stayed abroad for three years, lecturing in theology at the University of Paris, where he gained a great reputation for his scholarship. Recrossing the Channel in 1179 he soon gave proof that he had lost none of his zeal for reform; first he complained to the Archbishop of Canterbury about the bad table manners and the gluttonous habits of the Canterbury monks who had invited the returning archdeacon to dinner the previous evening. Next he interfered in the affairs of his sister, whose divorce from her husband he successfully thwarted. Back in Wales he soon discovered that the new Bishop of St David's had fled to England because his cathedral staff refused to obey him. Soon Gerald received a letter from Canterbury, authorising him to take over administrative responsibility for the diocese.

Five years later, in 1184, Henry II sent for him and made him a royal chaplain, which resulted in Gerald becoming a member of the king's retinue for the next ten years, for the first two of which he was seconded to the king's younger son, John who went to Ireland with Gerald as his personal chaplain. When Gerald returned in 1186 he found that London was agog with stories of awful happenings in the Holy Land where the infidel leader Saladin had succeeded in capturing the Holy Places in Jerusalem. Soon the king and Richard, his eldest son, along with the King of France, took up the cudgels on behalf of Christendom. Early in 1188 Henry II ordered the newly-appointed Archbishop of Canterbury to go to Wales to conduct a vigorous recruiting campaign to get volunteers for the Third Crusade; on the historic journey Archbishop Baldwin chose as his personal chaplain the Archdeacon of Brecon, Gerald the Welshman. The object of the journey around Wales was to preach the Gospel and to recruit volunteers, who would be ready to join an army, prepared to go to the Holy Land and do battle with the infidels who had captured Jerusalem. Those who took the cross were exempted from paying the 10 per cent tax imposed by the king to finance the expedition.

Baldwin, the leader, was getting on in

years, though not too old, it turned out, to go to the Holy Land, where he was to die in battle at the Siege of Acre; he was a son of the people, a Cornishman, who knew no Welsh and preached entirely in Latin. He needed all the assistance that his friend Gerald could give him. Gerald for his part, though of course able to speak Welsh, was fluent in Latin and French, generally choosing to preach in Norman French. The success of the enterprise depended on Gerald fulfilling a number of different functions: he was adjutant, public relations officer, interpreter and chaplain. He was of inestimable value to the party as he knew the areas, especially in southern Wales, through which they passed and invariably knew or was related to the leading people with whom they came into contact in the early weeks of the journey. In addition, once he had let out the fact that he had written two books, he was appointed by the Archbishop to be the official chronicler of the journey.

Gerald was a good travelling companion, as he was interested in a great many things and knowledgeable in most of them; he knew about animals and birds, he was conversant with local folklore, he was familiar with all the known mineral deposits, he was up to date with all the scandal attached to the families through whose fields they rode, he could discourse about ghosts and devils, he was able to put a name to every lake and mountain, and above all, he seems to have had a better than average sense of humour.

This journey began two days after Ash Wednesday on Friday 4 March 1188, the party riding out from Hereford on horseback, their main object to recruit as many Welshmen as possible to take the cross. In fact, approved volunteers were given a woven cloth cross, which after being blessed by the Archbishop was stitched to the right shoulder of the convert's coat. In seven weeks the party rode round Wales in a clockwise direction. In the first week they travelled via New Radnor, Hay-on-Wye, Llanddew (Gerald's home), Brecon and Abergavenny to Usk; the second week's itinerary was Caerleon, Newport, Cardiff, Llandaf, Ewenny and Margam to Swansea. After two nights in Swansea they progressed through Kidwelly, Carmarthen, Whitland and Haverfordwest to St David's, where three whole days were spent. On Monday, 28 March they set out again, visiting St Dogmaels, Cardigan, Lampeter, *Strata*

Florida, Llanddewi Brefi and Tywyn en route for Llanfair (near Harlech), where they arrived on 8 April. Thereafter Gerald was in unfamiliar country, as they passed through Nefyn, Caernarfon, Anglesey, Bangor, Conwy, Rhuddlan, St Asaph and Basingwerk to Chester, which they reached on Maundy Thursday 14 April. The three days of Easter were spent in Chester, before they left for Hereford, via Shrewsbury, Ludlow and Leominster, reaching their destination on Saturday 23 April.

Gerald kept a day-to-day diary on the journey; almost as soon as he returned he started writing the first draft of his book, based on what he had seen and thought about while away, but although he finished the draft in 1188, the completed book, written in Latin, was not ready for publication until 1191, by which time very many additions had been made to the text, including a reference to Baldwin's death which occurred in November 1190.

In all Gerald estimated that in the course of the journey more than 3,000 men took the cross, particularly successful recruitment returns coming from Hay-on-Wye, Abergavenny, Usk, Haverfordwest, Cardigan, Lampeter, Nefyn and Anglesey.

On their first stop at New Radnor, Gerald had been the first man to volunteer, thereby setting an example to the rest. At Abergavenny he related how a certain nobleman, whom Baldwin asked if he wanted to take the cross, replied, 'I cannot take such a step without consulting my friends'. The Archbishop retorted 'Ought you not to discuss the matter with your wife?' The nobleman at once answered 'This is man's work we are considering. There is no point in asking the advice of a woman'. So saying, without more ado, he joined the Third Crusade.

At their next stopping place, Usk, Gerald was amazed to find that many of the volunteers were 'robbers, highwaymen and murderers', while at Caerleon, he found time to wander in the Roman ruins, where he was enthusiastic about the 'immense palaces, which with the gilded gables of their roofs once rivalled the magnificence of ancient Rome'. Ten days later Gerald was in Haverfordwest, where he preached with some eloquence (he said so himself!) to a great crowd of interested people:

> Many found it odd and some indeed miraculous that when I, the

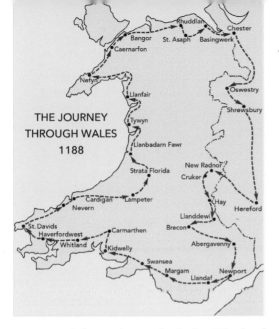

THE JOURNEY
THROUGH WALES
1188

jackdaws, who were so well looked after by the clergy that 'they never fly away from anyone dressed in black'.

Shortly afterwards, on a visit to Cardigan, where both Baldwin and Gerald preached, the latter referred to a particular incident, where a would-be volunteer was physically restrained by his wife, but a night or two later one of her children died, an occurrence she attributed to her action in holding back her husband, who was then encouraged to sign up, she herself in penitence sewing on the cross on his coat.

A few miles further inland at Cenarth, Gerald described in enthusiastic detail the dams in the river Teifi, made by beavers.

Later at Llanfair, on the coast near Harlech, he saw high mountains for the first time; he described the area as 'the rudest and roughest of all the Welsh districts'. 'The mountains,' he wrote, 'are very high, with narrow ridges and a great number of very sharp peaks all jumbled together in confusion. If the shepherds who shout to each other and exchange comments from these lofty summits should ever decide to meet, it would take almost the whole day to climb down and up again.' Then the party left for Bangor. They first went to the cathedral, where the archdeacon, preached the Word of God, speaking first in Latin and then in French, those who could not understand a word of either language, were just as much moved to tears as the others, rushing forward in equal numbers to receive the sign of the Cross.

At St David's, where the expedition stopped for three days, Gerald's chief comment concerned the cathedral's

Archbishop celebrated mass, assisted by the Bishop of Bangor; apparently before the end of the service Baldwin, in the presence of a large congregation, 'importuned, rather than persuaded' the Bishop to take the Cross. 'In the end there was nothing for it but that he took the Cross. This caused great concern to his flock assembled there, for both men and women present wept and wailed very loudly.'

A year after the journey finished, Gerald in the spring of 1189 crossed to France with Baldwin to join the crusade, but when in June Henry II died, his successor, Richard I, on advice from Baldwin, sent Gerald back home, being absolved from his vow in Dover on his way back to Britain. No sooner was he back from this dummy run than he settled down to writing his other book on Wales; this *Description of Wales* is invaluable because it represents what one man – and that one in a very privileged position, saw and believed in the twelfth century. It is divided into two parts, of which the first underlines the great virtues of the Welsh people, while the second discusses their failings.

After several chapters of a descriptive nature, which deal mostly with the physical geography of Wales, he turned to the people, whom he depicts as light in weight and agile, fierce rather than strong; everyone, it seemed, was ready to fight at a moment's notice. 'Sound the trumpet for battle and the peasant will rush from his plough.' Most Welshmen, we are told, lived almost exclusively on oats and dairy produce: milk, cheese, butter and beef. All Welshmen were devoted to freedom and the defence of Wales; as proof of their eagerness to right Gerald referred to a letter sent to Henry II by the Eastern Roman Emperor in Constantinople, who had enquired about the lives of people in Britain. Henry replied 'In one part of the island there is a race of people called the Welsh who are so brave and untamed that, though unarmed themselves, they do not hesitate to do battle with fully-armed opponents'. These Welsh freedom fighters spent little money on food and drink and clothes, concentrating on looking after their horses and keeping their weapons in prime condition. When not fighting, the Welsh were very hospitable, all their homes being open to all Welsh people. 'When a man is travelling away from home, he will walk into a house and hand over his weapons to the owner, who will give him water with which to wash his face.' This was regarded as a sign that he was a welcome guest. Both men and women had their hair cut short, and shaped round their ears and eyes; all men wore moustaches but not beards. Both sexes took great care of their teeth, which they were for ever cleaning with hazel shoots, before polishing them with woollen cloths until they shone like ivory. As to their wits, they were very intelligent, more so, according to Gerald 'than any other Western people'. They also had very able orators, who understood every trick and artifice of public speaking. They were too, readers will not be surprised to learn, very musical. 'When a choir gathers to sing, you will hear as many different parts as there are performers, all joining together in the end to produce a single organic harmony.' Furthermore, in all Welsh families an ability to play the harp was considered the greatest of all accomplishments.

Readers must find out for themselves about Welsh failings, such as those mentioned by Gerald in the second part of this book, but, though some of them sound startling and others unlikely to be true, in total they did little in Gerald's judgement to offset their virtues, of which he was always aware. At the end of the book he forecasts independence for Wales, by quoting the words of the Old Man of Pencader: 'I do not think that on the Day of Direst Judgment any race other than the Welsh or any other language will give answer to the Supreme Judge of all for this small corner of the earth'.

Scholarly though Gerald was, and a prolific writer too, he never lost sight of his main aim, which was to free Wales from the religious overlordship of Canterbury. Had he become Bishop of St David's, which remained his overriding ambition until 1203, he would have used his position there as the senior bishop in Wales to try to free the church in Wales from the authority of Canterbury. His ambition had survived his disappointment in 1176, when he failed to succeed his uncle as Bishop of St David's; in the 1190s the bishop's health deteriorated rapidly and once again the see was likely to be vacant. The strength of Gerald's obsession can be gained from the fact that at this time in quick succession the Bishops of Bangor and Llandaf died, and on both occasions Gerald refused the succession. The moment he was waiting for came in 1198, when the ailing Bishop of St David's died.

The next five years, 1198–1203, witnessed a remarkable struggle; these years constituted the climax of Gerald's life and ambitions. It should perhaps be stressed that for some time Gerald had held in veneration the memory of Thomas Becket, who had stood for the authority of the church against the increasing secular power of the throne. Had Gerald become Bishop of St David's, he would too have been willing, if need be, to be struck down in his own cathedral. Of these ambitions and intentions those who made Episcopal appointments were, of course, fully aware; nevertheless, Gerald was to maintain the struggle for five hectic years, when with all the cards stacked against him, despite many tribulations, he refused to give ground.

The campaign for a new bishop started in 1198, when the chapter of St David's submitted the names of four candidates to Canterbury, with Gerald's name top of the list; before a decision could be taken Richard I died, but his brother, John, who succeeded him, favoured the appointment of Gerald. John summoned Gerald to London, where in the presence of two canons of St David's he told Gerald that he proposed to make him bishop, but that he first had to win over the Archbishop of Canterbury. Gerald, much heartened by this unexpected turn of events, hurried down to St David's, where a full chapter elected him bishop and advised him to go at once to Rome, to be consecrated by the Pope, rather than to go to Canterbury for consecration there. Had this ploy succeeded, Gerald would have reached his goal; he would have obtained the bishopric and by being consecrated by the Pope would have established Welsh independence of the see of Canterbury. However, another four and a half years were to pass before St David's secured a new bishop and then his name was Geoffrey, not Gerald. To the amazement of all, Gerald accepted the verdict; by then he must have sensed the futility of further protest. With his immediate resignation as Archdeacon of Brecon he clarified his position; he was disengaging himself from the pursuit of further ambitions.

Gerald still had 20 years to live, years in which he mostly devoted his time to writing, though he did pay one more visit to Rome. When, in 1214, the see of St David's yet again fell vacant, he was not even prepared for his name to be put forward. By then he was living in Lincoln, where he was friendly with the great Bishop Hugh, who was rebuilding his cathedral after its virtual destruction in an earthquake. Little is known of Gerald's last years save that he died in 1223, when 77 years of age, and was probably buried in Lincoln.

Enough has already been written for the reader to sense Gerald's importance in his own generation; as the years went by, he became more Welsh than Norman in sympathies and outlook. He came as near as any man could in the circumstances of the day to slow down the pace of Norman expansion in Wales. Could he have achieved the separation of the Welsh church from the authority of Canterbury, the cause of Welsh independence would have been immeasurably strengthened. What cannot be gainsaid is that in his writings he left behind him an invaluable account of important aspects of life in twelfth-century Wales.

Changing fortunes under Llywelyn ap Iorwerth and Llywelyn ap Gruffudd

Again and again in this book some readers will probably note with surprise that a race as limited in numbers as the Welsh should be able in times of crisis to produce such outstanding leaders. The thirteenth century produced just such an occasion: the long drawn-out years of crisis were from the 1190s to the 1280s, a period that was covered by the lives of two men, Llywelyn ap Iorwerth – the Great – and his grandson, Llywelyn ap Gruffudd – the Last – the former being born in 1173, the latter dying in 1282.

In 1170, when Owain Gwynedd died, the outlook for Welsh hopes was not high, despite the fading of Henry II's plans for a successful resolution of his Welsh policy. A disastrous family squabble after Owain Gwynedd's death put paid to any realistic expectation for Welsh advancement in the immediate future. Then in 1189 Henry II died, to be succeeded on the throne of England by Richard I, whose short reign of ten years was almost exclusively devoted to the Third Crusade, thus offering the Welsh the opportunity for resurgence.

South of Betws-y-coed, the A470 runs into the delectable Lledr valley, where after a few miles the village of Dolwyddelan is reached under the southern slopes of Moel Siabod. Less than a mile (1.6 km) past the village, as the road begins to climb, on the right-hand side will be seen the ruined tower of Dolwyddelan Castle. Here in 1173 Llywelyn ap Iorwerth was born in what was probably the first stone castle to be built in this part of Wales. In this secure fortress, Llywelyn was to spend his boyhood years. Twenty years later he assumed a dominant role in the affairs of Wales, when he became ruler of Gwynedd, a position which he retained and strengthened in the following 40 years. At the time when he first achieved a position of power in 1194, there was an uneasy balance among the Welsh princes who opposed the invaders. The Normans, who from this time will be referred to as the English, controlled a large part of Wales, their writ running from Chester in the north-east to Pembroke in the south-west. Here the Marcher lords held sway. It should perhaps be stressed that at various times so great was their power and their influence that they acted as if they were independent rulers, who on occasion took action without reference to their feudal overlords in London. North and west of this English sphere of influence there were virtually independent Welsh rulers, who, unfortunately for the hopes of Welsh unity, frequently quarrelled with each other. The structure of English society was still feudal and many Welsh princes found it expedient, when there was a change of monarch in London, to travel there and pay homage to their nominal overlord.

Llywelyn, soon after taking over the reins of power in Gwynedd, found himself at variance with Gwenwynwyn, the ruler of Powys; theirs was always an uneasy relationship. In 1199, Richard I died and was succeeded by his brother John; Llywelyn paid allegiance to the new king, whose illegitimate daughter, Joan, he married in 1201. John, knowing of the rivalry between Gwynedd and Powys, attacked Powys, thus enabling Llywelyn to take advantage of his rival's troubles. He proceeded to annex territory in Powys, though before long the roles were reversed and Llywelyn found himself on the defensive against an alliance between John and Gwenwynwyn.

John, however, was by no means an astute king; he allowed himself the unwise luxury of quarrelling with more than one enemy at a time. His feudal vassals in

Fortresses of Welsh resistance to Norman occupation: 1. Carreg Cennen 2. Dolwyddelan; 3. Dinefwr

England, the barons, took issue with him at a time when the king was already embroiled with the Pope. In 1208, Innocent III lost patience and laid England under an interdict, which involved among other things the closing of all churches and a veto on Christian burial. Llywelyn, as much a statesman as a soldier, managed to get Wales freed from these prohibitions. Thus fortified, he continued to support the barons in England in their opposition to the king, at the same time planning the better government of the territories over which he ruled in Wales. He consolidated his position there by appointing skilled administrators to undertake the proper organisation of local government. Moreover the resultant improvement in the material welfare of his people in Wales was accompanied by a considerable cultural revival.

By 1215, John's struggle with the barons had come to a head, resulting in the king's submission at Runnymede. The privileges wrested from the king by Magna Carta were, thanks to Llywelyn's diplomacy, equally applicable to Wales. The following year saw the death of both his enemies, John and Gwenwynwyn; Llywelyn then called a meeting of all the princes of Wales at Aberdyfi, where Llywelyn's pre-eminence was recognised by all the princes, who accorded him the title of Llywelyn the Great, a title he had never sought for himself. In addition they all, great and small alike, pledged their allegiance to him. In 1216, therefore, Llywelyn the Great was the acknowledged leader of Wales, but in that year there ascended to the throne of England a man who was to put to the test all his qualities as diplomat and man of action, Henry III.

Late in the twelfth century the Cistercians, who had settled in successfully at *Strata Florida* in central Wales, sent out from there suitable missionary monks to found another house further north. After an initial attempt near Caernarfon, the monks moved on to the mouth of the Conwy river, where, on land given to them by the rulers of Gwynedd, Aberconwy Abbey was built. Today's visitors, who want to identify the site, are directed to the parish church in Conwy, whose chancel and nave survive from the former Cistercian house. Llywelyn took the abbey under his protective care, giving the monks a charter of clearly specified rights and privileges, and allocated land to them in the Conwy and Gwynant valleys.

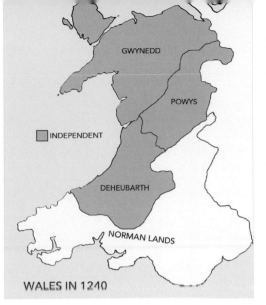

Llywelyn and Joan, it is believed, lived in Trefriw, from where on Sundays they climbed up to worship at the twin-naved church of Llanrhychwyn, above which looms the hill that fittingly bears its patron's name, Carnedd Llywelyn. This remote and historic church is still well worth a visit. Another tradition claims that in after years, when Joan found the steep walk up in to the hills beyond her reach, her husband caused a church nearer home to be built at Trefriw.

It is now clear, with the benefit of hindsight, that Wales was nearer to achieving her political ambitions in the first half of the thirteenth century than at any other time in the Middle Ages. In 1216 Llywelyn was at the height of his powers; in his early 40s, he was ready to flex his muscles, and an appropriate adversary had just become the King of England. The fact that Llywelyn chose to pay homage to Henry III indicated more than just the desire to be diplomatic by rendering a vassal's nominal obedience; he was in addition sending a signal to the English king to find out if he was prepared on certain terms to come to an understanding with the Welsh, just as Rhys ap Gruffudd had done with Henry III's grandfather 30 years before. At the same time, Welsh princes were being encouraged to marry into English baronial families. The stronger Llywelyn's own system of governing his scattered territories in Wales, the more likely, he felt, Henry would be to come to terms with him. Meanwhile, before putting the issue to the test, Llywelyn developed a form of executive government for the Welsh by calling councils of the princes who represented all the loosely-organised territories; at these meetings important

decisions were taken, dealing with such matters as settling boundary disputes and overcoming rivalries between differing factions. In fact, he was trying to cut right across tribal divisions, which in the past had again and again stood in the way of attempts to unify the country politically. He must certainly have made a very strong impression on his fellow princes by the business-like way in which he captured Norman castles in Shrewsbury, Llansteffan, Carmarthen, Aberystwyth and Cilgerran; the capture of the latter castle, inland from Cardigan, caused him to call another council of princes to meet him at Aberystwyth.

Henry III, alerted to the growing strength of his opponent in Wales, in 1231 moved westwards from Hereford to Painscastle, where for seven weeks in that summer the royal court was in residence. Painscastle today is well worth a visit; it is a very small village in Powys, 13 miles (21 km) west of Kington. Now it amounts to little more than a crossroads, a triangular green, an inn, a handful of houses and a

high green mound up a lane behind a farm in the very middle of the village. Over this place, however, for many a century loomed first a prehistoric strong-point, then a wooden castle, and later a stout, stone fortress. The mound on which a massive castle once dominated the scene is largely hidden by two farms that have been built between the eroded ramparts and the village. All is change; the hand of man is slowly withdrawing from the scene, but in the course of the century that followed the Norman conquest of England, Painscastle was constantly the scene of bitter confrontation between the invaders and the Welsh. Both sides at various times in this century, as in the next, occupied the area and the all-important hill.

In face of a renewed Welsh threat to the castle, the king moved his court there in 1231; that summer the castle was greatly strengthened and reorganised as a base for mounting a campaign of retaliation against Llywelyn. Interesting records survive of the king's activities there in that historic summer; in all 180 orders were promulgated from Painscastle on a variety of topics, both trifling and substantial. Of particular local interest was an order to the villagers to show more energy in

Cistercian abbeys founded by the Welsh princes: 1. Cymer Abbey near Dolgellau; 2. Strata Florida; 3. Talyllychau, Deheubarth

destroying wolves, which, according to the royal decree, were more numerous in that district than anywhere else in the kingdom. In Painscastle, Henry seems to have successfully shown the flag; two years later he again moved into Wales, from Hereford, this time in a south-westerly direction to Grosmont 14 miles (22.5 km) away. Grosmont is a large and very attractive village today, but at the time of the king's visit it was a considerable town, where a garrison of English troops were stationed. This royal progress to Grosmont in 1233, despite the apparent excellence of the castle's defences, ended in humiliating failure, as a surprise night attack by Llywelyn ended in its capture with the king and queen of England escaping in their night clothes, with some difficulty, to Monmouth, 10 miles (16 km) to the south of them.

Llywelyn, who had his sixtieth birthday the year he drove Henry III out of Grosmont, began to ponder about what would happen to his dominions after his death; Welsh history, he knew, contained many examples of dynastic quarrels about the succession to power when the ruler died. All too often, according to the traditional law of inheritance in Wales, estates were divided up at death and shared by members of the family, a process which invariably led to the proliferation of small estates and the spread of friction. With such thoughts uppermost in his mind, Llywelyn called what was to be his last council of princes, which met at *Strata Florida*, the great Cistercian monastery in central Wales. Today the abbey ruins are very well cared for, admirably set out for the enlightenment of visitors, whose historical interests are well catered for in a small but excellent museum on the site. Enthusiasts are advised, after leaving the grounds of the abbey, to wander through the churchyard next to the abbey, where they will probably marvel at the healthy yew tree that still burgeons above the grave of one of Wales' greatest poets, Dafydd ap Gwilym. At the council held there in 1240 Llywelyn successfully pleaded with the princes to recognise his son, Dafydd in due course to succeed him as ruler of Gwynedd.

Having gained this assurance Llywelyn then renounced his kingship and withdrew from public life and became a monk at the Cistercian abbey at Aberconwy, where he

Llywelyn the Great's statue at Conwy

died late in 1240. He was probably buried there but no one knows for certain, although in the parish church at Llanrwst, higher up the Conwy valley, will be seen a huge stone coffin, which holds a stone effigy of Wales' great leader. At his death most Welshmen probably believed that the necessary foundations had been securely laid on which those who came after him would be able to build an independent Wales. In 1240, national

hopes were very high, hopes that in the following 40 years were to be trampled into the dust of military defeat. Henry III, hearing of the accession to Llywelyn's throne of his inexperienced son Dafydd, took the offensive in an attempt as soon as possible to win back all Llywelyn's conquests. In 1246, only six years later, in the middle of this acute crisis for Gwynedd, the new king died. On Dafydd's unexpected death, there was the usual struggle for succession, which Llywelyn the Great had tried to prevent at the Council of *Strata Florida*. Dafydd's brother, Gruffudd, who had predeceased him, had four sons. Three of them strove to succeed their uncle as ruler of Gwynedd. Owain was the eldest, Llywelyn ap Gruffudd the second and another Dafydd the third; after nine years of fierce fratricidal infighting Llywelyn emerged as victor to become in 1255 the acknowledged ruler of Gwynedd, though in the process he had incurred the undying and politically damaging hatred of his younger brother, Dafydd. Llywelyn ap Gruffudd then took upon himself the awesome responsibility of standing up to a victorious Henry III. He soon succeeded in extending once again the authority of Gwynedd into central and southern parts of Wales, while Henry was faced, as his father had also been earlier in the century, by a serious revolt of the barons. The threat implicit in this new struggle, ably led by Simon de Montfort, prevented the king from giving his full attention to Llywelyn's activities in Wales. Meanwhile, Llywelyn continued the successful policy of his grandfather by giving all the help he could to the barons in revolt.

Henry, for his part, despite his involvement with the barons, deemed it expedient in 1257 to launch an attack against Llywelyn, but it proved unsuccessful. South of Welshpool lies the picturesque black and white village of Berriew, indicating the place where the river Rhiw joins the Severn. At a ford near there in 1257, Llywelyn ap Gruffudd stood his ground against the advancing army of the king, who was compelled to withdraw. Ten years later at the very same ford the two rivals met again, this time to sign a peace treaty. Between these two meetings much had happened to tip the scale in Henry's favour; the revolt of the barons had come to a disastrous end just two years previously in 1265, when their leader, Simon de Montfort, had been killed in the decisive battle of Evesham. In the Treaty of Montgomery in 1267, Henry recognised Llywelyn as the Prince of Wales, and accorded him a large measure of independence, in return for which Llywelyn agreed to pay him homage. 1267 stood out as the high watermark of Welsh political achievement to date; the King of England had actually recognised a Welshman as the Prince of Wales, a concession which meant that in future other Welsh princes would have to render fealty to the Prince of Wales, rather than as in the past to the feudal overlord in London. In addition, by the same treaty, Henry had handed over to Llywelyn a great deal of Marcher land, which for the previous 200 years had been in English hands. It is perhaps not surprising that for the five remaining years of Henry's reign, from 1267 to 1272, Llywelyn enjoyed real power in Wales.

Came the cold light of dawn in 1272; Edward I, who succeeded his father, Henry III, proved to be one of the strongest and most determined men ever to sit upon the throne of England. He was a man of quite outstanding political acumen and military ability; in addition he enjoyed an advantage, denied to his father, as he inherited from him a kingdom which for once was free from civil war and the threat of it. Seven years previously de Montfort's rebellion had been finally crushed at Evesham, thanks largely to the skill of the king's military leader, the Earl of Chester, which was the courtesy title of the future Edward I. Meanwhile, advance warning of future trouble was given to Llywelyn, when some princes, who had previously rendered homage to him, showed clear signs of allying themselves with the new king.

Llywelyn, in the very different political climate that followed the accession of Edward I in 1272, hastened to let the king know of his determination and his quality by building a stone castle at Dolforwyn, which stood on a ridge 400 feet (122 m) above the river Severn near Abermule in Powys. What remains of Dolforwyn castle (it has been in a ruinous state since 1398) may still be spotted by discerning enthusiasts who drive south from Welshpool. Clearly visible is the castle's walled enclosure, which measures 240 feet (73 m) by 90 feet (28 m). West of the site raised platforms and lumps in the grass still indicate where other buildings once stood. This fortress was intended to become Llywelyn's new capital, and as it stood only a few miles from the king's stronghold at Trefaldwyn, it sent a message to Edward that, while he, Llywelyn, intended to pay feudal homage to the king, he waited on his part for the king to reciprocate. That the king had no intention of making any reciprocal move was evident when he waylaid a ship en route from France and took prisoner its passenger, Eleanor, daughter of the dead and discredited Simon de Montfort, whom Llywelyn had announced his intention of marrying. To add to Llywelyn's difficulties, his younger brother, Dafydd, who for many years had bitterly resented his elder brother's succession to the Gwynedd estates, now formed an alliance with another of Llywelyn's domestic enemies, Gruffudd ap Gwenwynwyn, the ruler of southern Powys, an alliance which had as its sole purpose the overthrow of Llywelyn.

So much for the preamble to the war which Edward I declared on Llywelyn in 1276. The campaign was carefully planned by the king and depended on co-ordinated attacks from three of the royal castles in the west, Chester, Montgomery and Carmarthen, the intention being to lop off piecemeal the outlying territories ruled by

Llywelyn until he was driven back west of the Conwy river, to his own Gwynedd, when a systematic and concentrated attack would be mounted against him, if Llywelyn still stood out against the king. By 1277, the first part of his plan had been achieved, with the capture of Dolforwyn Castle; all was then ready for a major assault on Gwynedd. A royal army marched out of Chester, and at Rhuddlan was made ready for active service. The army then moved north-westwards to the north coast and cautiously made its way by easy stages until it reached the Conwy river at Deganwy. Meanwhile an English naval force had sailed westwards and landed in Anglesey, preparatory to destroying in the late summer, the harvest there on which Llywelyn's defending army relied for its provisions. Anglesey then, as in Roman times, was the granary of north Wales. Further south another English force, stationed in Carmarthen Castle, made for the west coast at Cardigan before continuing northwards to Aberystwyth. Llywelyn began to feel himself trapped west of the Conwy river and at the same time threatened by a pincer movement from the south; he therefore sought what he hoped would be temporary refuge in expediency by asking Edward for terms.

The outcome was the Treaty of Aberconwy 1277, which was a negotiated settlement to which Edward agreed because, although he certainly held the upper hand, his lines of communication were becoming stretched and he wisely wanted to conserve his resources. Nevertheless, although the treaty was no unconditional surrender, the terms imposed by the king were very severe indeed. Llywelyn had to agree to forfeit the allegiance of all Welsh princes, in return for which Edward allowed him to keep the title of Prince of Wales. In other words, to Edward, Llywelyn was no more than the feudal ruler of Gwynedd, the eastern boundary of which had to be the Conwy river. Furthermore, the king insisted that the reluctant Llywelyn should make his way to London, where he would have to perform his long-postponed act of homage to Edward. Llywelyn was back where he was before he signed the Treaty of Montgomery, with the additional loss of the territory between the Conwy and the Clwyd rivers to his alienated brother

Castles of dispute: 1. Llywelyn's castle at Dolforwyn; 2. Norman castle of Montgomery

Dafydd; he also had to hand back to the prince of Powys territory he had captured in southern Powys. Strangely enough, in the following year, Edward allowed Llywelyn at long last to marry Eleanor de Montfort. Even more strangely Edward and his queen attended the nuptials, which were celebrated with much ceremony and splendour in Worcester Cathedral.

In order to administer effectively the territories which Edward had taken from Llywelyn by the Treaty of Aberconwy, he sent into north Wales a great many officials, whose training for the tasks of local government had clearly not included any instructions about the need to take into account the susceptibilities of the people whose affairs they were sent to arrange. Wherever they went, these officials caused friction and resentment at a time when much tact and restraint were called for. By 1282, north Wales was once again seething with talk of open rebellion, which was fanned by the tactlessness of Edward's administrators. Llywelyn, for his part, by no means took kindly to defeat; the change in fortune from being the potential liberator of his people to becoming the tributary of his oppressor came too swiftly for him to digest.

Ironically, however, the spark that lit the dry tinder was supplied by Llywelyn's enemy in the recent war, his brother Dafydd, who was also suffering from the excesses of Edward's administrators in the lands which the king had taken away from Llywelyn and given to him. In bitter anger, Dafydd in 1282 attacked Edward's castle at Hawarden whose keeper, Roger de Clifford, had been made 'Justice of Wales' by Edward and was hated for his actions against the Welsh. This attack was by no means an unpremeditated act of revenge but formed part of a plan, intended later to involve attacks on other English strong points in northern and western Wales. Llywelyn, taken by surprise by his brother's aggressive act, at first stood aloof and did nothing, but as the struggle developed, he came to realise that if he was to continue as the chief protagonist of the Welsh cause he would have again to assume the leadership of the Welsh people against the English, despite the bad blood that existed between him and his brother.

The king, in reply to Dafydd's attack on Hawarden, pursued the same policy which had proved so successful in the previous war; his army advanced along the northern coast of Wales, while his fleet secured his

right flank before making for Anglesey. This time Edward met with much stiffer opposition; indeed, so very well did Llywelyn's men stand up to the English that he decided to hand over control in the north to his brother, while he took a small force into central Wales to rally support there and to try and recapture lost territory in that region. The stage was now set for the final scene, as Llywelyn moved southwards. The details of the tragic events of the early winter of 1282 are obscure – there are many differing accounts. Certain facts, have, however, been established: while Llywelyn's small force was laying siege to the royal strong point of Builth in central Wales, he slipped away a few miles to the south, where he owned a castle. The historically-minded are recommended to visit this area; a few miles south of Builth the river Edw joins the Wye at Aberedw, where on a well-wooded hill south of the village stood the castle, to which from time to time in the past Llywelyn had come for relaxation. In December 1282, he went there for the last time; soon he was advised to hide in a nearby cave, which still bears his name and is still with some difficulty accessible, unlike the castle, which for too long provided local builders with a free supply of building material. According to local tradition, while resting in the cave, word came to Llywelyn, inviting him to meet a Welsh deputation at an agreed rendezvous. Early one December morning Llywelyn broke cover, climbed down to the village and attended mass in the village church. Llywelyn, thus fortified, marched out to keep his rendezvous with fate; 2½ miles (4 km) west of Builth he was set upon and killed at Cilmeri, where an engraved stone commemorates the crime. His severed head was sent to the king. His body found decent burial near the high altar in the Cistercian monastery at Abbey Cwm Hir, a few miles north-east of Rhayader, where in 1982, on the 700th anniversary of his death, a wreath of remembrance was placed in the vestigial remains of the abbey by those who still hope to see Wales freed from all ties with England.

Meanwhile the struggle went on for another six months in the north where Dafydd assumed the leadership, but in June 1283 he was captured, taken to

1. Llywelyn ap Gruffudd's memorial at Cilmeri;
2. Abbey Cwm Hir

Shrewsbury and there executed, being the first to suffer the barbaric sentence of being hanged, drawn and quartered. With his death the war ended, and with it there died all hope of Welsh independence for another 100 years.

A word of warning may here be necessary, for, although Llywelyn and those who shared his views fought to get their freedom from any association with England, they were not animated by the sort of feelings which have inspired nationalists in modern times. A very strong sense of nationalism did undoubtedly grow up in Wales, but not as early as in the thirteenth century. Again it has to be stressed that Gwynedd's bitter disappointment at the overwhelming victory gained by Edward I was not by any means shared by all Welshmen; the wars that the two Llywelyns waged against the English mostly concerned Gwynedd. Indeed the princes of Powys and Deheubarth were Edward's native allies in the war against Llywelyn, while many other Welshmen had learned to live in reasonable comfort under the Crown and the Marcher lords. Nevertheless the price that the Welsh had to pay for not being able to agree with each other was very heavy, the first instalment of which being made apparent in 1284, when Edward I drew up the Statute of Rhuddlan. At Rhuddlan, Edward I set himself the task of disposing of the territories captured by Llywelyn and of arranging for the future government of north Wales; he also had it in mind so to organize the affairs of north Wales that in the future it would be exceedingly difficult for any Welsh leader to try to follow in Llywelyn's footsteps.

By the Statute of Rhuddlan in 1284, Edward I divided up Llywelyn's Gwynedd into three counties: Anglesey, Caernarfon and Meirionnydd, and appointed to oversee their organisation and maintenance an administrator with the title of Justice of north Wales. The land east of the former Gwynedd and west of Chester reappeared on the map as Flintshire, responsibility for the good government of which was added to the existing duties of the Justice of Chester. Similarly a Justice of south Wales was named to administer the affairs of the new counties of Carmarthen and Cardigan. Within each of the newly-created counties a sheriff dispensed justice, relying on a strange mixture of English criminal law and existing Welsh statutes which King

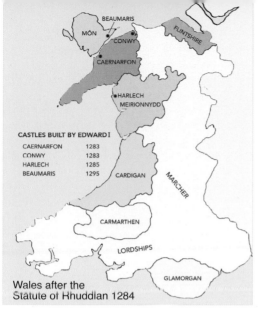

CASTLES BUILT BY EDWARD I

CAERNARFON	1283
CONWY	1283
HARLECH	1285
BEAUMARIS	1295

Wales after the
Statute of Rhuddlan 1284

Edward, thinking to pacify his Welsh subjects, was quick to point out were derived from Hywel Dda. Clearly there was no unified structure in the new system of government; much depended upon the whims and fancies of local officials. Nevertheless, respect for authority was rendered the more likely by the building of a chain of castles at strategic points in the new territories.

These castle afforded positive proof of the king's intention that his orders should be obeyed. The four main castles in the new counties of Caernarfon, Anglesey and Meirionnydd were built at Caernarfon, Conwy, Harlech and at Beaumaris. It is something of an irony of history that these superbly-built fortifications, whose sole purpose was to keep the local inhabitants in subjection, should have become major tourist attractions today, especially recommended by Visit Wales! First to be built was the castle at Caernarfon, which became the headquarters of the government of the three counties created in north-west Wales by the Statute of Rhuddlan. Begun in 1283 on a site on which the Normans had put up a motte and bailey, it took ten years to complete. From this vantage point Edward I tried to convince the Welsh people of his generous intentions towards them and hence, according to tradition, nominated his heir, the future Edward II, who had been born in the castle, as Prince of Wales, a custom, which was most recently observed in 1969, when Prince Charles was likewise invested as Prince of Wales in Caernarfon. At the same time as this prestigious castle was being built, some 1,500 craftsmen and their labourers were being employed in building another impressive strongpoint at Conwy, while further south, overlooking

Cardigan Bay, a third castle was begun in 1285 at Harlech on probably the best site of all.

Last of these masterpieces of medieval craftsmanship is still to be seen at Beaumaris in Anglesey, begun in 1295. The skill and labour of 2,500 men was needed to complete it. At Beaumaris, as at Caernarfon, Conwy and at Harlech, English immigrants were encouraged to settle, in each case providing a significant nucleus for a future town. It so happened that only a short distance from Beaumaris there was already in existence a small but thriving Welsh town, whose competition Edward I seemed to fear. In 1303, he arranged for the forcible removal of the entire population of Llanfaes to a new site provided for them in the west of the island, fittingly to be called Newborough.

Owain Glyndŵr: Hero of Wales

As has already been seen, by the settlement that followed the defeat of the last Llywelyn, the king ruled, through his agents, the counties of Anglesey, Caernarfon, Meirionnydd, Flint, Carmarthen and Cardigan. The rest of Wales, that is to say, the greater part of the country, was still controlled by Marcher lords, some of whom were Welshmen, who had at various times been richly rewarded for their services to the English crown. These Marcher lands were as much feudal domains as similar fiefs were in England. As a result of this feudal arrangement Welsh peasants had to work three days a week on their masters' lands, just as English peasants were compelled to do east of Offa's Dyke; however, early in the fourteenth century, many peasants, on both sides of the Dyke, managed to get their feudal lords to agree to let them pay rent for their houses on the lords' lands instead of having to work for them for three days a week. This gradual change may not at first have appeared very significant, although almost at once most peasants must have enjoyed for the first time some sense of freedom. After all, a tenant could hold his head higher than a serf. This change did not come about overnight, of course, but the tendency to exchange money payments for services on the land was greatly accelerated by events in the middle of the century.

In 1348 and 1349 the British Isles were

Glyndŵr's fortified courts at 1. Sycharth, Llansilin; 2. Glyndyfrdwy

visited by a fearful calamity, the spread of an epidemic of the dreaded bubonic plague, which in these two years accounted for the lives of about a third of the population. One immediate and inescapable consequence of the Black Death was a shortage of labour; hence the value of labour greatly increased. Peasants, freed from the shackles of serfdom, were able to sell their labour to the highest bidder. Parliament at Westminster, which above all at that time represented the interests of the landowners, in 1351 passed the Statute of Labourers in an attempt to put the clock back by refusing to recognise the legality of these wage rises. However, not even governments can fly in the face of economic facts, and after 1351 wages continued to rise. Thus, in the second half of the fourteenth century, the lot of most peasants in Wales, as well as in England, continued to improve. With this improvement went discontent and the demand for greater amelioration of their conditions. Revolutions are not made by men with empty stomachs, but rather by those with their stomachs half-full, who feel strong enough to increase their demands. Before the century ended in England, the peasants revolted, while in

Wales there was plenty of dry tinder around, just waiting for a spark to ignite it. That such a phenomenon as Owain Glyndŵr could arise in a country whose political ambitions and aspirations had been so recently and so thoroughly squashed, requires some explanation. Part of the reason lay in the personality and ability of the man himself, but part also has to be attributed to those social pressures which had been building up in Wales in the second half of the fourteenth century, following the impact of the Black Death and its drastic effect on the balance between landowners and labourers.

Visitors to north Wales today, who travel by road westwards from Llangollen on their way to Corwen, must first bypass the village of Glyndyfrdwy, which is pleasantly situated in the Dee valley and is much favoured by fishermen. All the land hereabouts once comprised a very important part of Owain's estate, his very name being a contraction of Glyndyfrdwy. He was born, however, on another family property, on the other, southern side of the Berwyn mountains at Sycharth, in the valley of Cynllaith, 1½ miles (2.4 km) south of Llansilin, south-west of Oswestry. The enthusiast today, Ordnance Survey map in hand, may still deduce from sundry lumps in the ground where once Owain Glyndŵr lived. He was probably born in 1359, the son of a man who was descended from the princes of north Powys and of a woman directly related to the rulers of Deheubarth in the south-west of the country. In addition he had a definite, though less direct kinship with the Llywelyn family, who had been masters of Gwynedd until 1282. In the course of the years Owain inherited from his father Glyndyfrdwy and Sycharth, and from his mother lands in the south, in Cardigan and Pembroke. He was most certainly born with a silver spoon in his mouth.

The young heir to such vast and important domains spent most of his boyhood years in Sycharth, where he enjoyed in splendid affluence the pleasurable activities, that comprised the usual and common lot of those whose fathers wielded power and authority in the Marches. Despite the extensive family property north of the Berwyn mountains in the Dee valley, where an important part of his adult life was to be spent, in his early years Sycharth was his home. It was from here that he went to London to complete his education. First he studied law at an

Inn of Court, as befitted an heir to great property, before taking up in earnest the profession of arms, in the following of which he achieved considerable distinction both for his appearance as a flamboyant and charismatic sprig of the aristocracy but also, and significantly, for his military prowess. He served in the army of Richard II (1377–1399) and took an active and honourable part in the battle of Berwick in 1385. His apprenticeship in arms once completed, he returned to his native land, where he seems to have migrated from Sycharth to Glyndyfrdwy, where he married Margaret, the daughter of Sir David Hanmer, who owned an estate in Flintshire. It was to prove a very fruitful marriage, Margaret bearing her husband no fewer than six sons and three daughters, but also a tragic one, as Owain was to be deprived in middle life of the company of all his family save for one son.

In 1400, the smooth and predictable prologue to Owain's career came to an abrupt and unexpected stop; action stations were at once taken up. Act One, Scene One of the drama proper of his life began in earnest.

Something needs to be said about the circumstances which suddenly caused the spotlight of attention to be switched on to the north Welsh town of Ruthin. Shortly before a combination of circumstances, both political and social, had brought about a clash between Owain Glyndŵr and his neighbour, a serious internal power struggle had taken place in London, as a result of which in 1399 the king, Richard II, had been made to abdicate by Parliament. They proceeded to put in his place on the throne of England Henry of Lancaster, who had by no means the strongest claim to the throne, even though he was the grandson of Edward III. This English dynastic crisis had serious repercussions in Wales because the outgoing King Richard II had many Welsh friends, including members of the Tudor family, which was at this time one of the most influential in Anglesey. Thereafter the Tudors, out of loyalty and friendship to Richard II, who was soon to be done to death in Pontefract Castle, adopted a hostile attitude to the new king, Henry IV. The latter, however, enjoyed much support among the Marcher lords, one of his closest friends being Reginald de Grey, whose forebears a century previously had received from the hands of Edward I the lordship of Ruthin, vacated by the Llywelyn family in 1282.

Some have called Edward I 'the Conqueror', but historians now view him as a tyrant. He spent incredible sums of money on hiring foreign mercenaries to invade Wales, followed by equally extravagant expenditure on building a chain of oppressive castles – the most expensive financial undertaking in Medieval Europe. England was already bankrupt before turning its attention to extending its occupation of Scotland and Ireland. The castle-building programme was followed by barbaric attacks on the Welsh population; large numbers of males were killed to prevent them from rising up in insurrection, and according to English records, hundreds of women, children and elderly people were also slaughtered. Taxes were increased sixfold in Wales after 1282, and in 1284 the first anti-Welsh legislation was passed: the Welsh could hold neither land nor office in any town, nor sell goods outside its walls; they were not allowed to carry arms or to testify against the English; Welsh was prohibited as a public language, and any Welshmen who were caught in town after dark would be executed without any recourse to a court of law.

Under such racist oppression – apartheid, in modern terminology – it was highly unlikely that even with the strongest network of castles, the Crown forces would be able to keep the Welsh in such a downtrodden condition for ever.

In 1400, de Grey picked a quarrel with his western neighbour, Owain Glyndŵr, who by this time had moved from Sycharth to Glyndyfrdwy; whereupon the disaffected Tudors, who were Owain's cousins, took the opportunity of showing their hostility to Henry IV by supporting cousin Owain's cause in his quarrel with the owner of Ruthin castle. In September 1400, with the quarrel between Owain and de Grey apparently beyond a peaceful solution, Owain's supporters met at Glyndyfrdwy and proclaimed their leader Prince of Wales. The die was cast, the gauntlet had been thrown down. Thereafter the quarrel developed into war between Owain Glyndŵr and Henry IV of England. The contest that ensued, touched off by a territorial quarrel between two landed gentry in north Wales and

Some of the Norman castles and colonial towns attacked during Glyndŵr's revolt: 1. Conwy; 2. Cricieth; 3. Harlech; 4. Caernarfon

supported on both sides for political reasons, unrelated to the local issues, soon broadened its base, as it attracted the attention of those with social grievances, whose chances of improving their position in society had been greatly enhanced by the shortage of labour brought about by the Black Death. The flames were also fanned by the ever-increasing hatred felt by a great many Welshmen for all things English, a hatred, which had spread rapidly since the infiltration of the Normans, who had decreed that the new towns that had grown up around the Norman castles should be exclusively inhabited by non-Welsh populations. Such towns as those in the shadow of the castles at Flint, Rhuddlan and Hawarden (there were others as well) were in the very first week of the uprising burned down by Glyndŵr's men. Owain's attack on Ruthin castle, which followed his proclamation as Prince of Wales, proved to be the military overture to a fierce campaign that lasted for ten years, a campaign which laid waste great areas of the country, destroyed many castles and churches and ended disastrously in total defeat for Owain Glyndŵr. And yet, for the very first time, a rising of Welshmen had enjoyed an overwhelming response from all classes in Wales, generating wild enthusiasm at the very real prospect of attaining national independence. This local quarrel in the north of the country then became a national uprising, which was also joined by many Welshmen who lived in England; they left their homes to hurry back to fight for the freedom of Wales.

Glyndŵr's revolt swiftly turned into a national war of independence, with the flames of the insurrection spreading to every part of Wales, and with military confrontation lasting for some 15 years. The effects of the conflict have continued to this day.

The initial tactics of the rebels were to strike hard and fast against the English towns, disappearing only to emerge in another part of the country, as huge armies from England were sent to look for them. Glyndŵr developed guerrilla tactics which are still studied by military strategists to this day. What with attacks by the rebels and reprisals by Crown forces, almost every town and village were destroyed during the fighting. Few houses in Wales today pre-date Glyndŵr's war of freedom.

In London Parliament's reaction to the speedy departure westwards of Welshmen, labourers and university students alike, was draconian; this sudden fierce outburst of anti-Welsh laws served only to increase the resolution of the Welsh and to inflame the more their hatred for the English. Owain Glyndŵr, for his part, after capturing Ruthin Castle, laid siege to the castle at Conwy, which he took in 1401, before moving further to the west along the coast, first to Bangor, where he set fire to the cathedral (because the Bishop supported Henry IV), and then to Caernarfon, where he besieged the castle. At this time his headquarters were high up in the hills, to the west of Snowdon, where in a secret retreat he recruited volunteers whom he then trained to become well-disciplined fighting men. Next he turned south and heavily defeated a stiff military challenge on the slopes of Pumlumon; by this time Owain was brimful of confidence as to the successful outcome of the struggle and called upon Welshmen everywhere to enrol under his flag, assuring them in a proclamation that he had been chosen by God to free his people from their English oppressors. From that time on Owain seems to have been here, there and everywhere, while the English military strategy was to play a waiting

game, protecting, wherever possible, their outlying castles.

In January 1402, Reginald de Grey of Ruthin petitioned his monarch, Henry IV, against any reconciliation of compromise with Owain Glyndŵr, despite their lack of success in the field. De Grey got his wish – the authority to occupy Glyndŵr's lands in their entirety. At the end of that month, Glyndŵr's retaliation came in the form of a second attack on Ruthin, slaughtering all who stood in his way, burning property and driving away the livestock.

Owain returned to Ruthin in April 1402, attacking the castle itself. De Grey was tricked into leaving the security of its walls and attempting to rush the Welsh, who fled to the hills where Glyndŵr's main force were in hiding. De Grey and his men fell into the trap and nearly all were slain. De Grey was captured and imprisoned by Owain at Dolbadarn Castle near Llanberis. A ransom note was sent to parliament in London – unless the sum was paid within four weeks, de Grey would be executed. A total of 6,000 marks were paid for his release in November 1402 and a further 4,000 for the release of his son at a later date. De Grey was released on condition he was not to raise arms against the

Welsh – something he never ventured to do again.

The events of that year favoured Owain Glyndŵr, with another successful battle being fought in Radnorshire in the valley of the river Lugg, a tributary of the Wye. The Welsh army, drawn up on the hill at Pilleth, above the church, waited for the English army, led by Edmund Mortimer, as it marched up the valley. The bowmen of Wales gave a good account of themselves, as they charged down the hill towards the valley, releasing their arrows at the English soldiery as they went. Mortimer, himself taken prisoner, lost a thousand men; the sequel, as events turned out, was to prove even more important than the battle, because Edmund Mortimer, in captivity, changed sides, a momentous decision which he celebrated by marrying one of the daughters of Owain Glyndŵr. Readers who want to involve themselves further in the battle of Pilleth are recommended not only to read Shakespeare but also to pay a visit to the delightful Lugg valley, which is south-west of Knighton. Here (GR 257683) up a long and grass-grown uphill lane, will be found Pilleth church, which is worth a visit for itself, especially as it possesses one of the few wells that still survive in a churchyard; here victors and vanquished may well have slaked their thirsts after the battle. Above the lonely churchyard (there is no village at Pilleth) may be seen on the skyline a clump of four redwood trees, which were planted to mark the graves of those who died there that day in 1402.

In the years from 1402 to 1404, Owain Glyndŵr carried all before him; the revolt had become a full-scale war for national independence, with the whole of Wales

The site of one of Glyndŵr's most memorable victories: Bryn Glas (Pilleth) in 1402

seemingly behind their leader except for those who lived in south Pembroke. These were the years, too, when Glyndŵr's adversary, Henry IV was beset by many problems, for, apart from having to try to contain Glyndŵr's revolt, Henry had to deal with recalcitrant barons nearer home as well as having difficult situations to attend to in Scotland, and in France. Hence, while Owain Glyndŵr was on the offensive, the most that the king could do for a while was to mark time until circumstances should alter sufficiently for him to be able to take the initiative. Even so, in 1403, while Glyndŵr was far from home at the head of his triumphant army, Henry IV's son, who was to succeed his father as Henry V in 1413, and later to defeat the flower of France at Agincourt, sacked Glyndŵr's two homes, at Sycharth and at Glyndyfrdwy.

1404 was the *annus mirabilis* of the revolt; in that momentous year Welsh armies seized and destroyed most of Cardiff, and laid siege to and captured Aberystwyth and its castle, before moving north against the mighty fortress of Harlech, which after some fierce resistance fell into Glyndŵr's hands. This feat, a very great achievement which showed the leader to be a man of outstanding military gifts, was soon followed the same year by the taking of political decisions, which pointed to his possession of equal gifts of statesmanship. On the morrow of this wholesale military success Owain Glyndŵr summoned a Welsh parliament to meet him at Machynlleth, which was thereafter named the capital of an independent Wales. It has already been seen how in 1400 at Glyndyfrdwy he had been proclaimed Prince of Wales by his friends, a title to which legal substance was now given by this gathering at Machynlleth in the presence of emissaries from France, Spain and Scotland. Thereafter Welsh ambassadors were sent abroad to serve Welsh interests in those countries.

Today in Maengwyn Street in Machynlleth will be seen the Parliament House, which was built in the sixteenth century on the spot where Owain Glyndŵr had called the first Welsh Parliament. In this historic parliament at Machynlleth, and in subsequent parliaments at Harlech and at Dolgellau, decisions of the utmost importance were taken. Where Giraldus Cambrensis failed, Owain Glyndŵr seemed to have succeeded; a Welsh parliament took the Church of Wales away from the jurisdiction of Canterbury, transferring responsibility to the see of St David's. Furthermore in future all Welsh priests were to speak Welsh and were to be educated and trained in Wales. To this end two universities were to be set up, one in north Wales and the other in the south of the country, where in addition to preparing priests for their vocations, Welsh civil servants were also to be trained to ensure the future good government of Wales. All these revolutionary changes were later ratified at another meeting, held at Pennal, near Machynlleth.

This then was the blueprint for the future government of Owain Glyndŵr's independent Wales. Had it ever been transferred from the drawing board to the statute book, there would have been a fair chance of a fundamental change in Wales but Thomas Huxley once defined a tragedy as a theory killed by a fact, and the stark fact was that Henry IV had time on his side, while he dealt piecemeal with his enemies at home and abroad. Then, freed from other worries, he was able to address himself to the tiresome problem of putting down what to him was an exasperating rebellion in Wales.

Meanwhile, Glyndŵr made hay while the sun shone; his headquarters were in Harlech Castle, where he lived with his wife Margaret, his six sons and three daughters, presiding over a court, which comprised many advisers, religious, political and military. For several years he lived there, the patriarch ruling his people, receiving deputations from abroad and sending out ambassadors far and wide. His chief military adviser was his former adversary, Edmund Mortimer, vanquished and taken prisoner at the battle of Pilleth, but now in 1405 installed in high office in Harlech, offering sound advice to his father-in-law. In addition to entering into an alliance with the French and starting negotiations with the Pope, Owain Glyndŵr, in these few precious years of power, signed in Bangor a Tripartite Agreement with Edmund Mortimer and the Earl of Northumberland, whereby after a joint successful war against Henry IV, his dominions were to be shared between Northumberland, Mortimer (who had a strong claim to the throne of England), and Owain Glyndŵr, whose Welsh boundaries were to be pushed out further to the east.

By 1405, however, the tide had begun

TRIUMPHS
OF
OWAIN GLYNDŴR
1401-1405

GLYNDYFRDWY

SYCHARTH

HARLECH

DOLGELLAU

MACHYNLLETH

ABERYSTWYTH

1401

1405

CARMARTHEN

1403

BRECON

1403

night attack. Of much greater military importance was another campaign, mounted by the future Henry V in 1408, when he laid siege to Aberystwyth, which he succeeded in taking after long and stubborn resistance. With gathering momentum, Henry's forces next moved northwards along the coast to invest Glyndŵr's headquarters and chief fortress at Harlech, where disaster was to strike for the Welsh in February 1409, when Mortimer died and the castle fell into English hands. In the ensuing pandemonium the victorious Henry took prisoner Glyndŵr's wife Margaret, and such children as were in the castle at the time, apart from one son, who managed to escape with his father. On that dreadful day of Welsh disaster, the cause was lost, even though Glyndŵr, almost alone, for some time continued the struggle. There were no more sieges or fixed battles, as Glyndŵr's following disappeared. The leader became a fugitive, who in 1410 was declared an outlaw. He passed into the shadows in 1412, when the last contact was made with him.

In the following year, 1413 Henry IV died and Henry of Monmouth became king as Henry V; the new king wanted peace in

to turn. Glyndŵr had probably overreached himself, his armies were exhausted, his treasury empty and his resources ominously stretched, at a time when Henry IV was beginning to plan his campaign to restore his authority west of Offa's Dyke. The military comeback of the English began in 1405, when Henry of Monmouth marched northwards 10 miles (16 km) to capture Grosmont castle in Gwent, which had been in Welsh hands since the 1230s, when Llywelyn the Great had taken the great fortress in a surprise

Wales, especially as war with France was thought to be imminent, but, although he twice offered a pardon to Glyndŵr, nothing was ever heard of him again. The rest is mystery and surmise, rumour succeeding rumour about where he was and what he was doing. All that can be said with certainty is that the most persistent of the many reports of his whereabouts alleged that he spent the rest of his life in the Golden Valley in Herefordshire, where those who give credence to these rumours believe that he was sheltered by his daughter Alice, who had married a Herefordshire landowner, Sir John Scudamore, and lived in Monnington Straddel, far from the prying eyes of men. But no one knows the time or place of his death nor where he was buried. Like a meteor Owain Glyndŵr blazed across the sky, leaving behind him a darkness more palpable than it was before.

Harsh English reprisals followed the collapse of the revolt; for years the clock was put back in Wales. That there was severe social and economic distress no man can deny, while the physical damage was there for all to see. Destruction of churches and castles was widespread, as armies both Welsh and English marched and countermarched up and down the country. Sir John Wynn in his *History of the Gwydir Family*, which he wrote in the 1580s, makes particular mention of the devastation to be seen in the Conwy valley, where he lived, which he attributed to Owain Glyndŵr's scorched earth policy, when defeat seemed inevitable. Modern historical opinion, however, thinks differently, attributing the ravaging of the Conwy and other valleys in Wales not so much to military as economic factors. The Black Death of the previous century had caused not only economic dislocation, but, by reducing the working population so drastically, had led to grievous rural depopulation.

Over the years much has been written about the place of Owain Glyndŵr in Welsh history but of one thing there can be little doubt. Those who today choose to underrate his importance are ill-advised. To a great many Welshmen, Owain Glyndŵr is the Father of Wales; he is their hero. The mere fact that there is no grave and therefore no visible proof of his death has done much to encourage the proliferation of legend. To him more than to any other must go the credit for making Welshmen conscious of their national culture and their national oneness; it has rightly been said that he lit a flame in the heart of his people that has never been put out.

Of modern writers about Wales no one has been more aware of Glyndŵr's lasting influence than Jan Morris, whose book *The Matter of Wales* was published in 1984; she thought of him as standing at her side. In the Prologue to her book she wrote: 'Owain Glyndŵr is present throughout the work, even when I do not mention him and, if he is hardly an unbiased monitor, he is certainly a mighty guide.' She calls him 'the most compelling of the emblematic heroes of the Welsh resistance'. Let the last word on Glyndŵr rest with a very distinguished English historian, G. M. Trevelyan, who, in his *History of England*, wrote: 'The wonderful man, an attractive and unique figure in a period of debased and selfish politics, actually revived for a few years the virtual independence of a great part of his country.'

Glyndŵr set out his vision for the future where Wales would have an independent church, two universities, a parliament and Welsh would be restored as an official language. He succeeded in maintaining his struggle for years against one of the richest nations in the world at that time. Although he never achieved permanent military victory, he kept his dream alive; subsequent generations inspired by him spent the next 600 years trying to fulfil his objectives. He is considered to be the father of Modern Wales, and his name and banner are seen throughout Wales today.

Notes and Illustrations

Giraldus Cambrensis and his contemporaries

Giraldus Cambrensis, born in the middle of the twelfth century, was a contemporary of Owain Gwynedd, who died in 1170, and of his own kinsman Rhys ap Gruffudd, who died in 1197. Gerald had much to say about these two Welsh princes, who between them had done much to control the destiny of Wales in this twelfth century. In 1188, in the later stages of his recruiting campaign for the Third Crusade, Giraldus, passing through Powys, came to the place where Henry II and his army had encamped in 1165, preparatory, they hoped, to launching an attack against Owain Gwynedd, whose army awaited an onslaught outside Corwen. Apparently, when the news reached Corwen that English soldiers had burned down a number of Welsh churches, the sons of Owain Gwynedd and many of their supporters were so incensed that they appealed to Owain Gwynedd to allow them to take a party of soldiers over into England to burn down English churches in revenge. Owain Gwynedd had the greatest difficulty, according to Giraldus, in holding them back, but finally succeeded in doing so, when he spoke thus to them: 'Unless we have God on our side, we are no match for the English. By what they have done, they have alienated Him. He can avenge Himself, and us too, in the most striking way. Let us accordingly promise God devoutly that from this moment on we will pay greater reverence and honour than ever before to all churches and holy places.' Giraldus then told his readers that it was on the very next day that the August storm blew up which forced Henry II to abandon his attack on Owain Gwynedd and to take his army back into England.

Two years previously in 1163, as has already been mentioned in the text, Rhys ap Gruffudd, the ruler of south Wales, had been tricked by Henry II and carried off to the royal court at Woodstock, where he became a prisoner. According to Giraldus, Henry II, meanwhile, in his desire to find out more about his captive, arranged for a Breton knight of his acquaintance to visit Rhys ap Gruffudd's home at Dinefwr Castle and to find out all he could about the place – its size, its value, the sort of crops it produced, its military importance, etc. The knight, a stranger to the district, in order to carry out the royal commission adequately, employed a local guide, who proceeded to lead his employer to the castle by a very rough and circuitous route, explaining as they went about the extreme poverty of the district, and the infertility of the soil, which compelled its inhabitants to eat grass. At this moment the guide reached down to the ground and, picking a handful of grass, pretended to eat it with great relish. Not surprisingly the report that eventually reached the king spoke of the backwardness of the area and the terrible poverty of its illiterate inhabitants. Henry II, giving proper credence to the report, allowed his prisoner to go back home, after extracting from him an oath of loyalty, which Rhys ap Gruffudd duly gave him, having been previously advised to do so by his shrewd uncle, Owain Gwynedd.

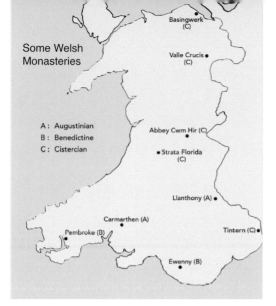

Some Welsh Monasteries

A : Augustinian
B : Benedictine
C : Cistercian

Basingwerk (C)
Valle Crucis (C)
Abbey Cwm Hir (C)
Strata Florida (C)
Llanthony (A)
Carmarthen (A)
Pembroke (B)
Tintern (C)
Ewenny (B)

Monasteries

Almost all the monasteries built in Wales in the Middle Ages were associated with either the Augustinians, the Benedictines or the Cistercians: the accompanying map will show the location of many of them, though the remains of some are vestigial, amounting in some cases to little more than foundations, as at Strata Marcella, near Welshpool. Benedictine and Cistercian houses were called abbeys, which were presided over by abbots, while the Augustinians built priories, whose

rulers were known as priors.

Something has already been written about these holy places in the text, where particular emphasis was laid on the great contribution made to life in Wales by the Cistercian order, three of whose abbeys will now be described, their selection justified, as will be seen, for quite different reasons: Abbey Cwm Hir in Powys, *Strata Florida* in Ceredigion, and Tintern in Gwent. Finally the Augustinian priory at Llanthony in the Honddu valley will be visited – it literally stands alone.

a) Abbey Cwm Hir (GR 056711)

Abbey Cwm Hir is remote indeed, being situated 5 miles (8 km) east of Rhayader in Powys and 8 miles (13 km) north of Llandrindod Wells; it can be reached by car by taking a left-hand turning off the A483, the Llandrindod to Newtown road. A minor reason for including Abbey Cwm Hir on the list of sites to be visited is the need to try to alert as many sympathetic visitors as possible to the acute problem of preserving what still remains. The masonry foundations of the Cistercian monastery benefited from a programme of conservation supported by Cadw during the 1990s. Those familiar with Cistercian settlements will expect to find Abbey Cwm Hir a long way from anywhere, and they will not be disappointed! The abbey and monastery were built in the middle of the twelfth century in a field at the side of the Clywedog Brook, a swift-flowing tributary of the river Ithon. In their early years the Cistercians abstained from eating meat; hence it became essential for them to settle near rivers, as fish formed a very important part of their diet. The builders came up from Whitland in south Wales, where Rhys ap Gruffudd had recently endowed a Cistercian house. It is perhaps difficult today, as one stands in the meadow by the stream, noticing here and there a broken pillar breasting a bed of nettles, to realise that the nave of the abbey measured 242 feet (74 m), a size exceeded only by the naves at Winchester, Durham and York. If Abbey Cwm Hir had even been finished, it would have been the largest abbey in Wales.

Barely a century after its dedication, Abbey Cwm Hir sided with Llywelyn ap Gruffudd in his determined stand against Edward I; when Llywelyn died near Builth in 1282, although traitors carried his head in triumph to the king in Rhuddlan, sympathisers took his body to Abbey Cwm Hir for honourable burial in front of the high altar. Another century passed and Owain Glyndŵr took up arms against England; although Cistercians sympathised with his cause, the abbey was destroyed in a raid by Glyndŵr's men in 1401. Thereafter there was only a limited amount of rebuilding; in 1542 came the final disaster, when surviving buildings were dismantled by order of Henry VIII's commissioners, but something of the architectural glory of the place may still be seen in the parish church of Llanidloes, whither in the same year six complete arches and much of the roof were skilfully and lovingly transported 10 miles over the hills from Abbey Cwm Hir.

b) *Strata Florida* (GR 747658)

In old maps a track, which ran westwards over the hills from Abbey Cwm Hir, led to *Strata Florida*; the existence of this link between these two Cisterican houses is not so surprising: the same Rhys ap Gruffudd of Dinefwr Castle (who founded Whitland Abbey, from where monks went forth to build Abbey Cwm Hir) also, in 1184 endowed *Strata Florida*, in whose abbey grounds he was eventually to be buried. *Strata Florida* is situated a mile (1.6

km) to the south of Pontrhydfendigaid and 2 miles (3.2 km) north of Tregaron. The surrounding district, still very sparsely populated, proved ideal for Cistercian settlement in the twelfth century, despite the lack of a river in the neighbourhood, which caused the enterprising monks to seek out local pools and to stock them with trout and eels.

Endowed in 1184, it was visited four years later, before it was finished, by Giraldus Cambrensis, who spent a night there as the guest of his kinsman, Rhys ap Gruffudd. Half a century later *Strata Florida* was again in the news, when Llywelyn ap Iorwerth, Prince of Gwynedd called an assembly of all the Welsh princes to meet him there. At this meeting he persuaded the princes to accept his son, Dafydd as ruler of Gwynedd, before retiring to become a Cistercian monk at Aberconwy Abbey, which had been established by monks from *Strata Florida*.

The main work of the abbey went on, day in, day out, despite interruptions from men and the weather (it was struck by lightning and seriously damaged in 1255); much land was wrested back from nature. Wheat and oats were successfully grown, peat was produced, fishing prospered, both in the mountain pools for eels and trout and in the sea for herrings. Above all, the monks of *Strata Florida* achieved real fame for their skill as sheep farmers. As early as in 1212 King John had awarded them a licence to sell and export wool. The end of monastic life there came suddenly, as elsewhere, when Henry VIII demanded the closure of all such houses of religion in the 1530s. Today *Strata Florida* is in the expert care of Cadw; the ruins are splendidly set out and suitably labelled, while there is in addition a small but really excellent museum.

Some readers may be interested in *Strata Florida's* connection with the stories associated with the Holy Grail; according to legend Joseph of Arimathea, escaping to Britain after the Crucifixion, settled in Glastonbury in the west country, having brought with him the very cup, carved from an olive tree, that had been used by Christ at the Last Supper; this is the Holy Grail of legend. Tradition insisted that for many centuries this precious relic stayed in the care of the monks of Glastonbury, until in the sixteenth century, when the Dissolution of the Monasteries was thought imminent, it was decided to take it to a place of safety, beyond the rapacious grasp of royal commissioners. Devoted monks are credited with having carried it over the hills for safe lodging at *Strata Florida*. After the dissolution reached even remote *Strata Florida*, the buildings passed into private secular ownership; in after-years members of this family moved from the former abbey to Nanteos, a mansion east of Aberystwyth, taking the Holy Grail with them. By this time the blackened wooden cup had acquired a great reputation for curing all sick people who drank their medicine from the cup. Again and again it was lent out to desperately sick people, who on returning the cup were required to put in writing their indebtedness to the relic. The most recent such letter is believed to have been written in 1903. Since then the family have left Nanteos and moved into Herefordshire, where the trail has gone cold!

c) Tintern (GR 535000)

Tintern lies about 5 miles (8 km) up the Wye from Chepstow, at a point where the river ceases to be tidal. The wild nature of this sparsely inhabited valley in the early twelfth century needs to be stressed because today Tintern is renowned for its idyllic setting in sylvan woodlands, which over the years have been much loved by poets and photographers.

The monks built their quarters at Tintern in 1131 but most of the splendid remains still standing are of the church which was put up by other monks 150 years later, the church being dedicated in 1288. It is this roofless church, rather than the monastic buildings, that excites the wonder of visitors today, and indeed sufficient of the thirteenth-century church remains to exemplify the excellence of the transitional architecture of the Early English and Decorated styles.

Nevertheless, attention must be drawn to the full range of monastic buildings still to be seen at Tintern, all of which are in various stages of ruin, including the cloisters (where much time was spent between services), the chapter-house (where daily meetings were held for confession and general discussions), the parlour (where monks might occasionally indulge in unsupervised conversation), the warming room (whose sturdy fireplace in cold weather blazed with a log fire), the refectory, the dorters (where the monks

Medieval monastries and abbeys: 1. Tintern; 2. Valle Crucis; 3. Basingwerk

slept), the kitchen, and the range of cellars. At a little distance, in a separate group of buildings are the remains of an infirmary, where they housed the sick and those who had served the order for 50 years.

Tintern Abbey in its prime was a large establishment, but it never acquired great wealth and in consequence it was as a lesser house that it was suppressed in the Dissolution in 1536. Nearly 350 years later Kilvert visited Tintern and noted in his diary in the last day of June 1875 that he climbed up on to the top of the walls, which were 'adorned with a perfect wild-flower garden of scarlet poppies, white roses, yellow stonecrop and purple mallow'. In 1901 the Crown bought Tintern from the Earl of Worcester, since when wonders have been worked to make it possible for twentieth-century visitors to realise what a great Cistercian monastery must have looked like in the Middle Ages.

d) Llanthony Priory (GR 288278)

Llanthony's much-photographed ruin is remotely situated about 6 miles (10 km) up the narrow winding Honddu valley in Gwent; it can be reached via the A465 Hereford to Abergavenny road, turning into the valley at Llanfihangel Crucorney, which is about 4 miles (6.5 km) north-east of Abergavenny. Giraldus Cambrensis, who knew the valley well, described it thus in 1188. 'The valley,' he said, 'is shut in on all sides by a circle of lofty mountains ... it is no more than three arrow shots in width.'

St David himself is credited with having established a *llan* there in the sixth century; the present church, built on the same site, dates from the thirteenth century and can be seen away on the left from the priory ruins; it is naturally dedicated to St David. To the ruins of this first church there came in 1103 a wordly Norman knight, William de Lacy, who had lost his way while out hunting; tradition has it that the Honddu valley was a Damascus Road to him. He apparently settled in the ruins, where he experienced a total conversion from his wicked ways and swore never to leave the place. Word eventually reached the royal court and Queen Matilda's chaplain, Ernisius, was inspired to join de Lacy in his retreat, where five years later the two men gathered around them a band of priests and together founded a monastic settlement. In 1118 this little community became Augustinian canons under their first prior, Ernisius himself.

These were troubled and unsettled times and the small settlement was often the victim of attack. Hence it was not until 1175 that the full range of ecclesiastic and monastic buildings was put up, to become one of the few Augustinian priories in Wales. The thirteenth century saw Llanthony in its prime; thereafter its decline was swift and, when dissolution came in the sixteenth century, the priory was small and poor. The last prior received a very small pension from the king, who handed the estate over to secular occupancy.

It passed from family to family until in 1790 a Colonel Wood acquired it; he turned the southern tower of the west front into a shooting lodge and converted the prior's lodging into a house. In 1807, the poet Walter Savage Landor bought the estate from him and came down to Llanthony with a grandiose plan for its future development, which never stood a chance of coming to fulfilment. Seven years later he went bankrupt and the dream faded away. Today happily the priory is in the public care, although the prior's lodging has become a small hotel, whose fortunate guests go to their bedrooms up a spiral staircase.

Since 1978 the Archaeology Department of Cardiff University has spent every summer season digging in the ruins at Llanthony; along with medieval skeletons have been found a great many artefacts, which include, in addition to animal, bird and fish bones, cooking utensils, roof tiles and slates, and needles and awls made of bone. There is no better illustration anywhere in Wales of a felicitous alliance between man and nature than here in the Honddu valley under the Black Mountains, where the present ruinous state of man's contribution in no way seems to detract from the overall effect.

Castles

When discussing early Norman infiltration earlier in the book, primitive castles were described, consisting of wooden keeps, erected on raised mounds, surrounded by fences of wooden stakes; these early strong-points were in time destroyed by fire or attack, and were replaced by rectangular stone keeps, or in some places by round stone constructions, known as shell keeps. This development in castle design was greatly changed in the reign of Edward I, who, in seeking to implement the provisions of the Statute of Rhuddlan of 1284, built huge concentric castles at strategic points like Conwy, Caernarfon, Beaumaris and Harlech, all of which were described in the text, making any further reference here unnecessary. In all the Normans built more than forty stone castles to contain the Welsh.

Also in this section attention will be paid to the stone castles that the Welsh themselves built for protection against Norman aggression. Four of these will be described, Dolwyddelan, Dolbadarn, Dinas Brân and Castell y Bere. There were others, such as those at Ewloe, Dolforwyn, Dryslwyn and especially Dinefwr, which will be dealt with separately later in this book.

In the southern Marches, in Gwent, there survive three Norman castles, which were originally erected after the Conquest to protect the Norman stronghold of Monmouth, namely Grosmont, White Castle and Skenfrith; as all are within easy each of each other and are accessible to the public, some details will be given.

a) Dolwyddelan Castle (GR 722524)

Towards the end of the twelfth century the Welsh took a leaf out of the Norman book and, imitating the Norman way of building castles, constructed stone fortresses for themselves at strategic points. An early example, built in about 1270 may be seen in the upper part of the Lledr valley, high up on a rock, a mile (1.6 km) beyond the village of Dolwyddelan. Its builder was Iorwerth Drwyndwn (Iorwerth of the Broken Nose), whose facial deformity was thought by some to be responsible for his being passed over for the full inheritance of the Gwynedd estates. Instead he received as his portion Nant Conwy, which he proceeded to fortify at Dolwyddelan. Here, according to tradition, his son Llywelyn ap Iorwerth, destined to become Llywelyn the Great, was born; he certainly spent most of his boyhood there.

b) Dolbadarn Castle (GR 585598)

Another of these early Welsh castles may be seen in a dominant position in the pass of Llanberis on the west shore of Llyn Padarn. The surviving tower, some 40 feet (12 m) high, serves to indicate to today's visitor something of its importance in the Middle Ages. It was probably built by

Dolbadarn castle

Llywelyn ap Iorwerth, whose grandson Llywelyn ap Gruffudd chose to imprison there his elder brother Owain Goch (*Owain the Red*) for upwards of 20 years. A younger brother Dafydd lived there for a while until the Earl of Pembroke captured the castle for Edward I. More than a century later Dolbadarn Castle was back in Welsh hands because in 1401 Owain Glyndŵr imprisoned there his enemy Lord Grey of Ruthin, until the requisite ransom was paid.

c) Castell Dinas Brân (GR 224433)

Castell Dinas Brân was built in about 1270, probably by Gruffudd ap Madog, the son of the founder of the Cistercian Abbey, *Valle Crucis*. It occupied a most commanding position 750 feet (228 km) above Llangollen, and about three-quarters of a mile (1.2 km) north of the town, across the river Dee. Visitors to Llangollen will know how the ruins of the castle, perched on the crown of the hill, and silhouetted against the sky, dominate the view. The castle, however, had a short and chequered history; built on the site of an Iron Age hill fort, some of whose ramparts remain, it seems to have been abandoned less than ten years after it was built, a fire in 1277 having proved disastrous.

An excursion to Llangollen, which takes in Eliseg's Pillar and the nearby *Valle Crucis* Abbey, as well as Castell Dinas Brân, all north of the river, is much to be recommended, especially if the weather is kind and the day is rounded off with a call at Plas Newydd, where the Ladies of Llangollen lived for 50 years.

d) Castell y Bere (GR 660086)

This ruined castle is well-hidden, inland from Tywyn in Gwynedd; it is best

Castell Dinas Brân

castle to fall to Edward I. After the death of Llywelyn ap Gruffudd in 1282, the struggle continued for a while under his brother Dafydd, who held out at Castell y Bere, from which he managed to escape when finally it fell. The castle was abandoned by the English in 1294.

Few historical sites convey so strong a sense of the past as does this twelfth century stronghold, built by the mighty Llywelyn ap Iorwerth; magnificently situated under Cadair Idris, it commands from its highest ramparts, to which a path leads from the road, incomparable views in all directions.

The Trilateral

e) **Grosmont** (GR 405244), its geographical setting implicit in its Norman-French name, owes its existence to this fact because the Normans saw the defensive possibilities of the big hill towering above the river Monnow. In 1201, King John entrusted Hubert de Burgh with the task of replacing the wooden keeps of the three castles of the Trilateral with sturdy stone ones. The new stone castle at Grosmont became the most important of the three; hence a prosperous town grew up there to supply its needs. Today

approached from Tywyn, following the narrow-gauge railway, which ends at Abergynolwyn. Turn left here on to a minor road, which leads past the ruins on its way to Llanfihangel-y-Pennant. This is an outing for the connoisseur, who does not mind the hazards of narrow lanes, with an escort of buzzards overhead! Here, in this deserted upland area, once stood a stout outpost of Welsh resistance to Edward I. Indeed Castell y Bere, whose ruins are partly obscured by trees today, had the distinction of being the last Welsh

Grosmont is no more than a large village with a population of about 500, but the bare bones of a spacious medieval town are still visible in the former burgage plots of land, where the lord's tenants built their cottages and grew their food. This planned medieval town was cruciform in shape, with the road from the castle running down to the church, which was also built in the thirteenth century. Crossing this road at right-angles was another road, the village high street today, where most of the medieval building took place. This medieval town acquired the status of a borough with the attendant privileges of holding fairs and markets.

All that remains today of the thirteenth-century castle are the gates to the inner bailey beyond the wooden bridge that spans the deep moat, the massive eight-sided chimney above the banqueting hall and two drum towers on the enclosing walls. Twice in its turbulent history the castle changed hands; early on in the thirteenth century its newly-built defences were tested and found wanting when Llywelyn ap Iorwerth made a surprise and successful attack in the middle of the night, when Henry III and the entire court were in residence. Henry and Queen, Eleanor made a hasty and undignified escape in their night attire. Thereafter Grosmont remained in Welsh hands until 1410, when the English recaptured it from Rhys Gethin, who was defending the castle for Owain Glyndŵr.

f) **White Castle** (**GR 380167**) The apex of the defensive triangle was an isolated hill, where a motte and bailey was built in the eleventh century, known as Llantilio Castle; subsequently rebuilt in stone by Hubert de Burgh, it was covered with a coat of white plaster, which caused it to be thereafter called the White Castle. It was in its heyday in the late thirteenth century, when it was enlarged and much strengthened. By 1275 it had real military importance. As at Grosmont, there was a civilian settlement, of which today there is no trace at all save for grass-covered lumps in the ground and references to burgage plots in local records.

Today White Castle stands impressively alone; no castle in Wales gives a more immediate sense of power. Thanks to Cadw the castle today, though in ruins, offers a clear picture of life in the thirteenth century. The outer bailey, which is very extensive, is surrounded by curtain

walls with drum towers at the corners; beyond that is the gatehouse with its two circular towers, which gives access to the inner bailey, the nerve centre of the castle. Along the walls of the inner bailey may be seen the kitchen, the oven, the hall, the well, the solar and, in the south-east corner, the chapel. Nowhere is the basic military purpose of a Marcher castle more marked than at White Castle, which is calculated to make a striking visual impression on the imaginations of the young. A historically-minded parent would do well to start his children's initiation into the pleasures of looking at castles by showing them the solitary splendour of White Castle.

g) **Skenfrith** (GR 458203) Skenfrith castle, the third castle of the Trilateral, looms over an attractive village beside the river Monnow, 3 miles (4.8 km) south of Grosmont. Skenfrith, like White Castle, failed as a planned medieval town, the place never seeming to have amounted to more than a castle, a church and a cluster of cottages of various styles and sizes, which today happily comprise a peaceful and delightful village. Skenfrith is Celtic in origin. In Welsh it is called *Ynysgynwraidd*, 'the island of Cynwraidd', thought to have been a local chieftain.

The castle's strategic importance arose from its proximity to the river, the crossing of which at that point it was able to control. Skenfrith was the last of the three castles to be rebuilt and strengthened, but records show that in 1241 the new stone castle received important if incidental additions, such as oxen for ploughing, crossbows, extra kitchen utensils, and a supply of wax for lights in the chapel. Skenfrith, properly equipped, was thought to be capable of withstanding attack from any quarter, but in the event it seems that it was never put to the test. The castle in fact has enjoyed a peaceful and uneventful history ever since.

The approach to the castle from the village street is impressive because the curtain wall through which access to the castle is given via the vestigial traces of a gate-house is almost at its original height; these four curtain walls enclose the courtyard and have drum towers at all four corners. In the middle of the courtyard

1. Aberteifi (Cardigan) castle and bridge; 2. Castell y Bere; 3. Strata Florida *Abbey*

stands a round tower, built upon a mound, similar to one behind the manor house at Tretower in the Usk valley. Originally the castle was surrounded by moats on the north, south and west sides, linking up with the river Monnow, which provided protection from the east. Today only the gentle slope of a dry moat remains; there is nothing visible to convey the sense of isolation suggested by a ditch 7 feet (2 m) wide and 9 feet (2.7 m) deep. Here at Skenfrith is an unpretentious but perfect outline of a thirteenth century castle, to which nothing has since been added to blur the idea of what a small Marcher stronghold of those distant years really looked like.

Owain Glyndŵr

It is unfortunate that so little can still be seen that is connected with Wales' greatest hero. He inherited two estates, one at Glyndyfrdwy, in the Dee valley between Corwen and Llangollen, the other, the larger of the two, is on the other side of the Berwyn mountains at Sycharth, in the valley of Cynllaith; even in his lifetime his enemies destroyed both of his homes. Certainly in Machynlleth, where he exercised real power, the Parliament House survives, but in fact this is a later building, occupying the site of his Parliament House. Owain Glyndŵr has his memorials elsewhere, in the hearts and minds of his fellow countrymen.

To those who venerate Glyndŵr's memory a pilgrimage can still be made to a remote hillside in Montgomeryshire, a few miles west of Oswestry, where (GR 204258) a mound may be identified, which, in Shakespeare's words, is 'girdled by its moat of shining water', beyond which are substantial ramparts.

Glyndŵr's memory as a national hero: 1. Statue at Corwen; 2. Parliament House and 3. Glyndŵr Centre at Machynlleth

Towards Union – or Annexation

The Tudor Triumph

The fifteenth century had dawned bright and clear for those Welshmen who saw Glyndŵr as the saviour of his people, who, they thought, would lead them to freedom and to nationhood. But by the end of its second decade it had turned sour. There was darkness in the land, as news of English repressiveness reached Welsh ears. The penal code was first decided upon by Parliament in London in 1401 and 1402, when Glyndŵr's revolt began to gain momentum. Among the severer penalties to be exacted was a veto on Welsh possession of land in or near towns, and on the holding of any office under the Crown. In addition, intermarriage between the Welsh and the English would involve the English partner being made subject to the same restraints as the Welsh. It has to be said, however, that from the time of the death of Henry IV in 1413 the code was never rigorously applied except briefly in exceptional circumstances in 1430 and 1447, but the very existence of such measures on the Statute Book did much to exacerbate the already bitter relationship between the Welsh and the English. It is of some interest to note that the lack of job opportunities for ordinary Welshmen led to their enlistment in large numbers in the English army, as readers of Shakespeare's *Henry V* will bear testimony.

Attention has now to be diverted to the Welsh family of Tudor, whose future was to be inseparably linked with the fortunes of the throne of England. The earliest member of the family, according to the chroniclers, was Ednyfed Fychan, who had been steward to the Gwynedd estates, when the great Llywelyn ap Iorwerth held sway; two sons of his continued to serve Gwynedd in the same capacity up to the time when tragedy overtook the fortunes of Llywelyn ap Gruffudd in 1282. Despite the misfortunes which followed the death of this Llywelyn, the Tudor family continued to prosper, as it is known that in the middle of the fourteenth century one Tudur ap Goronwy was a very considerable landowner, who at his death handed on to his eldest son Goronwy a property in Anglesey, known as

Penymynydd. The grandsons of this Goronwy supported their cousin Owain Glyndŵr in his great uprising. If the death of Llywelyn ap Gruffudd had done little to diminish Tudor fortunes, the same cannot be said about the sequel to Owain Glyndŵr's failure. Tudor properties were confiscated and Rhys, one of the cousins, was executed in Chester in 1412, while his brother Maredudd seems to have escaped into obscurity.

Although Maredudd's later career was wrapped in mystery, that of his son was indeed remarkable. To start with, he had been christened Owain after his distinguished uncle Glyndŵr; yet as a very young man he was to be found in the employment of the royal court of Henry V, where as a page he was made to anglicize his name to Owen and to add an English-style surname, for which he chose Tudor (rather than Maredudd). In 1422, his royal master died, leaving his queen, Katherine of Valois, a widow and a nursing mother at 20; by a change of fortune, which must subsequently have astounded many generations of Welshmen, this young kinsman of Owain Glyndŵr married the widow of a king of England!

In the middle years of the fifteenth century the long drawn out Hundred Years' War with France came to an end and, with it, the return to England of large numbers of trained English fighting men, more work for whom was soon to be provided at home in the Wars of the Roses, which were to bedevil the lives both of England and Wales for almost the rest of the century. From this time on, Wales played a very important part in the unfolding and troubled drama of English political history. A great dynastic struggle was threatening the English crown, a struggle which on the return of the English armies from the continent turned into a bitter civil war, whose ramifications even 600 years later are too complicated to be satisfactorily unravelled. It is enough to say that two families had competing claims to the throne of England, the Yorkists and the Lancastrians. Wales, despite its repeatedly professed desire to be freed from any connection with England, was yet deeply involved, indeed never more so than in the Wars of the Roses.

To return briefly to the affairs of the Tudor family, the marriage of Owen Tudor and Henry V's widow, Katherine, prospered and produced four children, a daughter and three sons, two of whom were to figure prominently in the history of the fifteenth century. The boy-king Henry VI, who succeeded his father, Henry V, in 1422, looked with favour upon his half-brothers, making Owen Tudor's eldest son, Edmund, Earl of Richmond and his younger brother Jasper, Earl of Pembroke. Furthermore in the fullness of time the king arranged the marriage of Edmund to Margaret Beaufort, who was the great-great-granddaughter of Edward III. This Earl of Richmond died at Carmarthen in 1456, but early in the following year his 14-year-old wife, Lady Margaret Beaufort, gave birth to his posthumous son, Henry Tudor, who by virtue of his mother's distant connection with Edward III, became a claimant to the English throne.

When hostilities broke out in 1460, Wales seems to have been about equally divided in its loyalties; the Lancastrian heartland was in the west and south of the country, where Jasper Tudor, the Earl of Pembroke, loyally supported his half-brother, the Lancastrian king Henry VI. The Marches, on the other hand, where ran the writ of the Mortimer family, were mostly Yorkist in their sympathies. In 1461 the head of the Mortimers, the Earl of March, who had some Welsh blood in his veins, and who had in William Herbert a Welsh chief of staff, defeated a Lancastrian army, which contained a great many Welshmen. Many of them lost their lives that cold February morning at the Battle of Mortimers Cross in Herefordshire (Owen Tudor was taken prisoner and executed in Hereford). As a result of this battle the young earl marched to London where he was proclaimed king as Edward IV, to the exclusion of the Lancastrian king, Henry VI. This division of Welsh loyalty and the general Welsh involvement in the war illustrates the difficulty faced by Welshmen, like Owain Glyndŵr, who so recently had tried so hard to divorce Wales completely from English affairs.

After the accession of Edward IV in 1461, following his success at Mortimers Cross, the Welshman William Herbert quickly rose to a position of great eminence under the new Yorkist king; later that same year he was made Chief Justice of South Wales, becoming Lord Herbert. In 1467 he was also appointed Chief Justice of North Wales and ordered in 1468 to lead an expedition into Gwynedd to take Harlech Castle from

Jasper Tudor, who was defending his last stronghold. Again Herbert triumphed; he then marched his army back to England, where his brief but brilliant career came to a sudden end, being defeated with his Welsh supporters at the Battle of Banbury in 1469 and afterwards executed.

Of all the supporters of the Lancastrian cause in Wales two men stood out, Jasper Tudor, the Earl of Pembroke and Rhys ap Thomas, head of the Dinefwr family. Jasper Tudor, after his defeat at Harlech, led a chequered life for some years. First he took self-inflicted exile in France, and then returned to England, until the Lancastrian defeat at Tewkesbury in 1471 ended for the time being all Lancastrian hopes, making it necessary for him to return to his French exile. This time he took with him his 14-year-old nephew, Henry Tudor, Lancastrian claimant to the throne of England.

The other great Welsh champion of the cause, Rhys ap Thomas, was head of a family whose founder was Rhodri Mawr himself, who in 876 had announced his plans for a united Wales. Again and again in the Middle Ages this family had taken the lead, Rhys ap Tewdwr in the eleventh century and Rhys ap Gruffudd, the Lord Rhys in the twelfth. The latest scion of the house, Rhys ap Thomas, born in 1449, made contact with young Henry Tudor in exile and promised him his full support when circumstances should allow him to return to Wales.

Back in England Lancastrian hopes were falsely raised in 1483 when the Yorkist king Edward IV died. These hopes were dashed when the throne was seized by the dead king's brother, Richard III, who proceeded to appoint as his right-hand man in Wales a great Marcher lord, the Duke of Buckingham, who owned vast estates in Powys. Later in 1483, in October, a Welsh rising was planned to coincide with the long hoped-for landing in Wales of Henry Tudor and his army. Unfortunately for Welsh dreams the elements took a hand; Henry's fleet was scattered in a storm and forced to return to France, while the Duke of Buckingham, who had recently defected from the Yorkist to the Lancastrian side, was cut off by the river Severn in spate, captured by his enemies and executed. On Christmas Day in France Henry Tudor, in an impressive ceremony in the cathedral in Rennes, rallied his followers and restored their spirits by swearing a solemn oath that when he had defeated Richard III and secured the throne of England he would bring civil discord to an end by marrying the daughter of Edward IV, Elizabeth of York. During these 14 long years of Henry's exile in France, Welshmen had been fed stories of the youthful Henry who would one day, their bards assured them, wear the crown of England. Many were the tales told of the great promise shown by Henry, causing him repeatedly to be referred to as a second Arthur and even another Glyndŵr.

On 1 August 1485 the 28-year old Henry Tudor once again set sail from France, this time accompanied by an army of 2,000 men, which landed at Dale, near Milford Haven, on the evening of Sunday 7 August. No time was wasted, as on the Monday the invading army passed through Haverfordwest before spending the night at Nevern. Next day, gathering recruits as they went, they marched through Cardigan, heading north along the coast to the river Dyfi, which they crossed near Machynlleth on Thursday 11 August. Then they turned east and made for the hills; on Saturday 13 August Henry's army crossed the river Severn at Welshpool and then pitched camp on the Long Mountain (*Cefn Digoll*). The Long Mountain seems to have been the prearranged meeting place for Welsh detachments to join the main invasion force. It is known that here the Lord of Dinefwr, Rhys ap Thomas, joined Henry, bringing with him a formidable fighting force, which he had raised in south Wales. A letter was sent by Henry Tudor to Welsh magnates, inviting them to take part in the great venture. Henry's army, by the time it left the Long Mountain, was very much swollen in numbers and was accompanied by a substantial supply train. It then marched eastwards through Shrewsbury, Stafford, Rugeley, Lichfield and Tamworth to Market Bosworth, where Richard III barred the way. On Monday 22 August was fought the Battle of Bosworth, just 15 days after Henry Tudor had set foot on Welsh soil.

Though heavily outnumbered, Henry's forces gave a good account of themselves; the battle was fierce and decisive with Rhys ap Thomas dealing the coup de grâce to Richard III and being rewarded, according to tradition, by the immediate award of a knighthood by the new king, Henry VII. Twelve days later Henry rode in triumph into London, where at the end

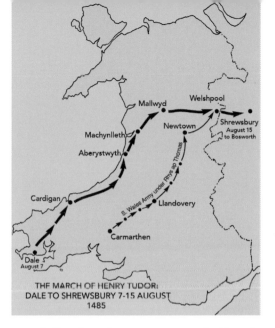

THE MARCH OF HENRY TUDOR:
DALE TO SHREWSBURY 7-15 AUGUST
1485

past to try to see the events under consideration through the eyes of those alive at the time; to judge the history of one country, or one society, by the standards of another invariably leads to doubtful judgments being made. And so it is with the immediate events that preceded and followed the accession of Henry VII. There are those who today maintain that everything unpleasant that has since befallen Wales and Welshmen should be attributed to the accession of a Welshman to the throne of England, and that Wales had had to pay dearly for Henry Tudor overconcerning himself, as they see it, with the affairs of England.

At the time Welshmen reacted differently from the English to the outcome of Bosworth. To the latter it was a matter of relief that at long last the bitter civil war had come to an end. To Welshmen, however, Henry Tudor's victory was a glorious affair, because it meant to them that the long struggle between the Welsh and the English had resulted in a Welsh victory, with a Welshman seated thereafter on the throne of England. Most of Wales celebrated Henry's victory at Bosworth and his accession to the throne.

of October he was crowned. Shortly afterwards he was married, as he had promised, to Elizabeth of York, the sister of the young princes who had been done to death in the Tower of London. This political marriage really does seem to have achieved its purpose of reconciling Lancastrians and Yorkists, even though twice in Henry's reign unsuccessful attempts were made to rekindle the flames of civil insurrection.

It is always as well when reviewing the

Henry Tudor was but 28 years old when he became king, having spent all his adult life abroad in exile, where he had of necessity to learn how to adopt a cautious approach to life and also how to harbour his very limited resources. His personality may have been reserved and he certainly never courted popularity, but he was a patron of learning and a lover of music. He did see to it that fellow countrymen who had contributed significantly to his success were suitably rewarded. His right-hand man at Bosworth, as well as receiving a knighthood on the battlefield, enjoyed great advancement: Sir Rhys ap Thomas became Constable and Steward of Brecknock, Chamberlain of Carmarthen and Cardigan, indeed becoming the virtual ruler of south Wales. In addition in later years he played a crucial part in putting down the revolts associated with Lambert Simnel and Perkin Warbeck. In his last years he lived in great state at Carew Castle, where a great tournament was held to celebrate his award of the Garter. Many other Welshmen acquired high positions in church and state, at least four of them becoming bishops. The anti-Welsh penal laws passed by Henry IV early in the fifteenth century were of course held in abeyance. The young king shows how aware he was of his high standing in Wales, when he christened his first-born son, Arthur, later reviving for him the title of Prince of Wales; it is interesting to note in this connection that Thomas Malory's *Morte D'Arthur* was printed by Caxton in the very year of Henry's accession.

Although a Welshman was now King of England, Wales was not, of course, a part of England. The political structure of Wales had developed in an ad hoc manner in the previous 400 years as the Norman invaders and their successors had sought to make inroads into the lands on the western side of Offa's Dyke. The Wales, for the good government of which Henry VII became responsible in 1485, consisted of two distinct and different parts. First there were the Marches, where, since the Conquest, vassals infeudated by the king had become so powerful – and were so far from London – that at times they resembled rulers of independent lordships. An attempt to bring back these Marcher lordships under central control had been made by Edward IV, who set up a Council of the Marches. The other political division of Wales had come about at the end of the thirteenth century in the reign of Edward I, after the death of Llywelyn ap Gruffudd and the seizure and redistribution of his lands. Edward created a principality, which consisted of six shires, Anglesey, Caernarfon, Meirionnydd, Flint, Cardigan and Carmarthen.

By and large Henry VII made no dramatic alteration to the government of Wales; in the Marches he revived Edward IV's Council of the Marches, to whose headquarters in Ludlow he later sent his son Arthur, when he reached his fifteenth birthday, at the same time buttressing his authority there with trusted Yorkist advisers, whose task it was to offset local Welsh rivalries. This council became the bridge between central authority in London and the Marches, but after Arthur's untimely death in 1502 his successor as Prince of Wales and heir to the throne chose not to set foot in Ludlow. Good Welshman though undoubtedly Henry VII was, he was unable to make any significant change in the direction of Welsh affairs, so heavily did he become immersed in matters of state.

The Act of Union 1536

Henry VIII succeeded his father in 1509. He was too preoccupied for 20 years and more with weighty matters of state to spare a thought for Wales. But in the middle 1530s he authorised his chief minister, Thomas Cromwell, to turn his attention to the growing needs of Wales. Indeed, between 1485 and 1536 it had become increasingly obvious that the existing pattern of authority in Wales, both in the counties created by Edward I and in the Marcher lordships, was at best clumsy, and at worst quite inadequate. This was especially so in the Marches, where the separate lords behaved like independent potentates, with their own laws and courts. By this time, too, these lordships covered a very large area indeed, having extended their borders far into west Wales. Throughout these territories disorder had spread, so that some change had to be made to prevent mere disorder turning into absolute chaos. This unsatisfactory state of affairs seems to have been known by everybody except Henry VIII, who did nothing to ease the Welsh situation until circumstances forced his hand in the 1530s and made him instruct Thomas Cromwell to reorganise the whole government of Wales.

It is interesting to speculate upon the reasons which prompted the king so belatedly to make himself concerned with the state of Wales. Henry was not a man to feel any pang of conscience at the neglect of his fellow countrymen in Wales, nor is he likely to have listened to pleas from Welshmen to take heed of their grievances. The truth is that the radical changes that were brought about by the settlement of 1536 have to be seen etched against the background of the general history of a momentous decade, at the beginning of which Cromwell had succeeded Wolsey as the king's chief adviser. Thanks to his abiding devotion to Henry's political ambition to make himself an absolute monarch, Cromwell orchestrated the total breach with the Pope, as a result of which Henry was able to obtain his divorce from Catherine of Aragon and make himself the head of the Church of England. Cromwell then proceeded to bring all the revenues from the monasteries, which were being confiscated at that time, into the royal coffers. The result of these actions was that the king became the very powerful ruler of a modern national state. To add to the centralised power, Cromwell soon gave his royal master firm control over Wales in 1536, when parliament under his tutelage passed the Act of Union. Drastic measures were deemed necessary in London to prevent the recurrence in the future of any threat to English domination in Wales, such as those associated with the risings made in the names of Llywelyn ap Iorwerth, Llywelyn ap Gruffudd, and by Owain Glyndŵr.

The changes brought about by Thomas Cromwell were indeed fundamental, amounting in the opinion of many to surgery without anaesthetics. As far as the Marcher lordships were concerned, they were simply abolished and in their place were created counties. Some of the existing counties, which had come into existence in the settlement of Edward I a century and a half previously, were considerably enlarged as former Marcher territories were added to them, but five new counties were created as well, Monmouth, Brecon, Radnor, Montgomery and Denbigh. All Welsh counties thereafter sent members to the Westminster Parliament, the knights representing the counties and the burgesses the towns.

The general principle was also established in matters of law that the laws of England should prevail at every level of Welsh life, thus scrapping every vestige of

Welsh law. In every county new courts of law were to be set up, which would be empowered to try the less serious breaches of the law. More serious crimes like murder and robbery were left to the jurisdiction of higher courts, provision for which was made by dividing up Wales into four circuits, which judges were to visit twice a year. These were known as the Great Sessions of Wales and lasted until 1830.

Having arranged for lower courts of law to be set up in all the counties, Cromwell had then to find suitable administrators to bring them to life. He thereupon introduced into Wales the system of voluntary Justices of the Peace, a system which had been developing successfully in England since the fourteenth century. Justices of the Peace in England – and, after 1535, in Wales – were responsible for seeing that reasonable government was maintained at the local level. Local gentry became virtually the nominees of central government; their chief sphere of influence was the Quarter Sessions, which, meeting four times a year, became the governing bodies of the counties, where all judicial (below the level of serious crime),

executive and administrative decisions were taken. These Justices of the Peace enjoyed an enormous range of powers, becoming virtually policemen, judges and civil servants. It has now to be seen where in Wales such invaluable local officials were to be found.

Until the fourteenth century in Wales, when a man died, his property was equally divided between his heirs; this process of inheritance operated in a very different way from primogeniture in England, whereby the oldest son inherited his father's estate. The consequence of gavelkind in Wales was that no strong rural middle class could come into being. From about the middle of the fourteenth century, however, the Welsh had started to practise primogeniture, with the result that gradually the desired middle class began to grow and the gentry that resulted began to assume political power as their affluence increased. In addition, many members of the gentry either followed the law or indulged in trade, which made them richer and therefore more important members of their society. By the 1530s the Welsh gentry were deemed strong enough to be entrusted by the government in England, with the responsibility of administering the local affairs of Wales as laid down in the Act of Union. At the same time some Welsh families benefited considerably from the distribution of the material wealth of the monasteries, whose dissolution began in the same year as the Act of Union was passed. Tudor legislators in London soon saw the political wisdom of cultivating the trust and friendship of the Welsh gentry, from whose ranks Justices of the Peace were selected, while the gentry, who now built themselves splendid houses and sent their sons to Oxford, came to realise that it had a vested interest in the survival of the Tudor dynasty on the English throne. In other words, this new Welsh class and the Tudor rulers in England came to an understanding, and thereafter shared a very important community of interest.

The Council of the Marches, which Edward IV had revived and which Henry VII had made use of, was now expanded to become the Council of Wales, which, in the absence of any Welsh capital acceptable to all Welshmen, was again centred in Ludlow, where it virtually became the centre of the government of Wales, becoming the headquarters of its legal and administrative life.

Seeing that the Act of Union seemed at the time to have been acceptable to the Welsh people, who gave no visible sign of opposing it, many Welsh people clearly took Henry VIII at his word when he said that his object was to give equality of opportunity to the Welsh. It has then to be asked why in after-years have so many Welsh people held the Act of Union responsible for every ill that has since befallen their country. One of the provisions of the Act insisted that English was to be the only language to be spoken in the new law courts, Welsh judges and Justices of the Peace being required to conduct their business solely in English. Such a request presented no difficulty to the newly-empowered Judges and Justices of the Peace, because educated Welshmen were bilingual, but obviously as the Judges on circuit began to try their cases and the Justices of the Peace made their pronouncements in Quarter Sessions, those who knew only Welsh were at a very serious disadvantage. Furthermore, this insistence on the use of the English language meant that, if Welshmen sought advancement, they had to concentrate on learning English, thus neglecting their native tongue, which was accordingly downgraded, to be used only by the underprivileged. As things worked out, in the course of time, the Welsh ruling class, which had been given power in 1536, became thoroughly anglicized and increasingly remote from any affinity with the bulk of their fellow citizens. The sense of injustice of this language provision in future years did much to increase the hostility the Welsh felt for the English: hostility that has been further inflamed by a growing awareness of national identity, which has followed the spread of nationalism in the twentieth century.

However fair the 1536 settlement appeared to many Welshmen at the time (and the language barrier took some time to do its damage), there were, even in 1536, some Welshmen, the spiritual heirs of the two Llywelyn and Owain Glyndŵr, who did not want their country to be indissolubly linked with England. Both Llywelyn and Glyndŵr may have seemed rebels to the English, but they were – and still are – heroes to the Welsh. English people, who today live in Wales, should be well aware of the passionate attachment of Welsh-speaking Welsh people to their language and their culture. My fellow countrymen, who on occasion have been very insensitive to Welsh sensibilities, would do well to remember that, as has truly been said, sometimes history is the propaganda of the victors.

Notes and Illustrations

Henry Tudor

Having landed in south Wales early in August 1485, Henry required all the help he could get. Accordingly, he wrote to the leading men of Wales, demanding their immediate assistance. The following is an excerpt from one of these letters:

> Right trusty and well-beloved, we greet you well ... through the assistance of our loving friends and true subjects, and the great confidence that we have to the nobles and commons of this our Principality of Wales, we ... in all haste possible descend into our realm of England ... we desire and pray you, upon your allegiance, strictly command and charge you that ... with all such power as you may make defensively arrayed for the war, you address yourself towards us without any tarrying upon the way until such

time as you be with us, wheresoever we shall be, and that you fail not hereof as you will avoid our grievous displeasure and answer unto it at your peril ...

In provisioning his rapidly-growing army, Henry, once he reached Machynlleth, was able to take advantage of the drovers' routes. Since the early Middle Ages droves of cattle had been driven from their Welsh pastures to the markets of England. Not only was Henry able to march along the drovers' tracks over the moors, he was also able to buy cattle en route from the drovers to feed his hungry troops, especially between Machynlleth and Shrewsbury. These drovers' routes were to be regulated by statute in the following century, soon after the Act of Union.

Dinefwr Castle (GR 611 218)

The keep of this ruined castle still stands high up above the river Tywi, which it dominates a mile (1.6 km) or so south-west of Llandeilo, in Carmarthenshire. This castle, along with Dryslwyn and Carreg Cennen, in former times controlled the Tywi valley. It was here that the mighty Rhodri called a conference in 876, at which he outlined his plans for the unification of

Dinefwr Castle

Wales. In 1080 the castle was held by Rhys ap Tewdwr, but it was towards the end of the twelfth century that Dinefwr was at its peak of importance, when Rhys ap Gruffudd, the future Lord Rhys, was its master. In the following century Henry III sent an army of English soldiers up from Carmarthen to lay siege to Dinefwr: all in vain, as it turned out, as 3,000 Englishmen were killed, along with their leader. In 1276 however the English did succeed in capturing the castle and for a while an English garrison was established there. In

Dryslwyn Castle

Brown. In Victorian times the mansion acquired the Gothic front, which still adorns the family home of the Dinefwr family. In the grounds will be seen fallow deer and a priceless herd of white cattle, which are reputed to be the descendants of the long extinct wild cattle.

The Act of Union 1536

Interpretations of the Act of Union have varied considerably but what may not be disputed are the actual words of the Act:

> the country of Wales justly and righteously is ... incorporated, annexed, united and subject to and under the imperial Crown of the Realm, as a very member and joint of the same.

the fifteenth century Rhys ap Thomas, Henry Tudor's chief lieutenant in Wales, who later received a knighthood on the field at Bosworth, returned to Dinefwr as the king's viceroy in south Wales.

In the sixteenth century the castle was allowed to fall into ruin but a splendid mansion was built there in the grounds. Thereafter a succession of additions were made to the house and great improvements were also made to the gardens, which in the eighteenth century received the attention of Capability

Bibliography

The Journey Through Wales, Gerald of Wales (Penguin Classics)

Historical Atlas of Wales, J. Idwal Jones (University Press, Cardiff)

Owen Glendower, J. E. Lloyd (O.U.P.)

The Matter of Wales, Jan Morris (O.U.P.)

South Wales and the Marches 1284-1415, W. Rees (O.U.P.)

An Historical Atlas of Wales, W. Rees (Faber and Faber)

Wales Through The Ages Vol 1, ed. by A. J. Roderick (Christopher Davies)

Wales Through The Ages Vol 2, ed. by A. J. Roderick (Christopher Davies)

History of the Gwydir Family, Sir John Wynn (Gomer Press)

By the same author:

Wales Before 1066 – a guide (New edition)
Wales After 1536 – a guide (New edition)
Radnorshire – A Historical Guide
Country Churchyards in Wales

Welsh place names

Anglesey *Ynys Môn*
Brecon *Aberhonddu*
Breconshire *Sir Frycheiniog*
Cardiff *Caerdydd*
Cardigan *Aberteifi*
Carmarthen *Caerfyrddin*
Chepstow *Cas-gwent*
Denbighshire *Sir Ddinbych*
Glamorgan *Morgannwg*
Grosmont *Y Grysmwnt*
Holyhead *Caergybi*
Knighton *Trefyclo/Trefyclawdd*
Lampeter *Llanbedr Pont Steffan*
Laugharne *Casllwchwr*
Monmouth *Trefynwy*
Monmouthshire *Sir Fynwy*
Montgomery *Trefaldwyn*
Montgomeryshire *Sir Drefaldwyn*
New Radnor *Maesyfed*
Newport *Casnewydd*
Offa's Dyke *Clawdd Offa*
Radnorshire *Sir Faesyfed*
Rhayader *Rhaeadr*
Ruthin *Rhuthun*
Skenfrith *Ynysgynwraidd*
St Asaph *Llanelwy*
St David's *Tyddewi*
St Dogmael's *Llandudoch*
Strata Florida Ystrad Fflur
Swansea *Abertawe*
Tenby *Dinbych-y-pysgod*
White Castle *Castell Gwyn*
Whitland *Hendy-gwyn ar Daf*